THE RITES OF KNIGHTHOOD

The New Historicism: Studies in Cultural Poetics
STEPHEN GREENBLATT, GENERAL EDITOR

THE RITES OF KNIGHTHOOD

THE LITERATURE AND POLITICS OF ELIZABETHAN CHIVALRY

Richard C. McCoy

University of California Press
Berkeley · Los Angeles · London

University of California Press
Berkeley and Los Angeles, California

University of California Press, Ltd.
London, England

© 1989 by
The Regents of the University of California

Library of Congress Cataloging-in-Publication Data

McCoy, Richard C., 1946–
    The rites of knighthood: the literature and politics of Elizabethan
chivalry / Richard C. McCoy.
        p.   cm.—(The new historicism: studies in cultural poetics: 7)
    Includes index.
    ISBN 0-520-06548-4
    1. English literature—Early modern, 1500–1700—History and
criticism.   2. Chivalry in literature.   3. Chivalry—History—16th
century.   4. Knights and knighthood in literature.   5. Knights and
knighthood—Great Britain—History—16th century.   6. Politics and
literature—Great Britain—History—16th century.   7. Great
Britain—History—Elizabeth, 1558–1603.   I. Title.   II. Series: New
historicism: 7.
PR428.C45M34   1989
820'.9'353—dc 19   88-36946
                                                                                    CIP

Printed in the United States of America

1   2   3   4   5   6   7   8   9

To My Mother and Father

Contents

Illustrations

Acknowledgments

This book has taken a long time to write, and I have a number of funding agencies, institutions, and individuals to thank. I began the project while on a research grant from the National Endowment for the Humanities several years ago, and I finished writing the final chapters while on leave with the assistance of a grant from the American Council of Learned Societies. Several travel grants from the Research Foundation of the City University of New York enabled me to return to England to continue archival research. That research proved very rewarding, and I am grateful to the librarians and archivists at a number of collections for their invaluable assistance: Robert Yorke at the College of Arms; Richard Luckett, Pepys Librarian at Magdalene College, Cambridge University; Kate Harris at Longleat House; Andrew Prescott at the British Library's Department of Manuscripts; Norman Evans at the Public Record Office; Robin Harcourt Williams at Hatfield House; and Robert Babcock at the Beinecke Library, Yale University. I also relied on the collections of the University Library at Cambridge University, the Columbia University Libraries, and the Folger Shakespeare Library. The Society of Fellows at Columbia University provided me with a study and extended opportunities to discuss my work during my research leaves. I benefited greatly from participation in the Folger Institute's seminar on Elizabethan political thought, run by Professor Donald Kelley.

Several friends and colleagues have read this work, or portions of it, at various stages of its development, and I would like to thank them for their encouragement and useful criticisms: Simon Adams, Jeffrey Alexander, Paul Alpers, Sir Geoffrey Elton, Julian Franklin, Stephen Greenblatt, Richard Helgerson,

Arthur Kinney, F. J. Levy, Wallace MacCaffrey, Charles Molesworth, David Norbrook, Annabel Patterson, David Starkey, Joseph Wittreich, and two members of the Editorial Committee of the University of California Press. I am also grateful to those who offered useful advice—Vincent Crappanzano, Ron Levao, Louis Montrose, Linda Leavy Peck, Kevin Sharpe, and Sir Anthony Wagner—and to those who provided indispensable practical assistance—Jonas Barish, Dean Helen Cairns, Wm. Theodore de Bary, Jean and Richard Gooder, Loretta Nassar, Lena Cowen Orlin, Janet and Nick Pott, and Dean Jack Reilly. My wife, Marsha Wagner, offered intelligent criticism and advice, practical assistance, and moral support while pursuing her own hectic schedule. Our children, Kate and Sarah, have been wonderful companions, especially during our travels to England. In the spirit of gratitude they inspire, I dedicate this book to my own parents, Hugh and Betty McCoy.

Introduction

In the opening scenes of Shakespeare's *Richard II* Henry Bullingbrook, Duke of Herford, accuses Thomas Mowbray of treason and challenges him to single combat:

> By that, and all the rites of knighthood else,
> Will I make good against thee, arm to arm,
> What I have spoke, or thou canst worse devise.[1]

My book concerns the cultural practices and literary texts of Elizabethan chivalry, and the opening scenes of *Richard II* convey a vivid impression of chivalry's ritual solemnity and vigor. These scenes also reveal the tensions latent within chivalric ceremony, foreshadowing the more open antagonism between the King and his powerful noble subjects. I have chosen *The Rites of Knighthood* as my title because it is a typically pointed Shakespearean pun, showing how the rites of judicial combat are informed and driven by a belief in knighthood's inviolable rights.[2] By his challenge, Bullingbrook declares his grievance before the King and demands satisfaction in a fair fight: "What my tongue speaks, my right drawn sword may prove" (I.i.46). The King's disruption of these proceedings is made to seem an almost sacrilegious violation of chivalric ritual as well as an intolerable abuse of the rights of knighthood. Richard continues to abuse the "royalties and rights of banish'd Herford" (II.i.190) by seizing the latter's inheritance, and Bullingbrook returns to England to reclaim his title and his lands. Denied the vindication of his rights within "the chivalrous design of knightly trial" (I.i.81), the Duke defies the King to regain them by open revolt. Their contest ends with the deposition and murder of the King, crimes that in turn lead to civil war.

1

In Shakespeare's later history plays, the Wars of the Roses thus originate in a mortal conflict between the nobility's "customary rights" (II.i.196) and the power of "right royal majesty" (II.i.120). A similar conflict persisted in Shakespeare's time, muted and unresolved for much of Elizabeth's reign but erupting violently at its end in the revolt of the Earl of Essex. In fact, *Richard II* was explicitly linked to the revolt because the conspirators commissioned a performance of the play the night before, on February 7, 1601, hoping its scenes of courtly corruption and tyrannous abuse would rouse the London populace to join them in armed insurrection. Their hopes were disappointed. The badly organized rebellion failed, and the Earl was arrested and executed on February 24.

The Earl of Essex was a heroic paragon of Elizabethan chivalry, admired for his brave and reckless exploits in battle as well as his dazzling appearances in the Accession Day tilts, the annual tournaments celebrating the Queen's accession to the throne. For many of his contemporaries, his tragic downfall made him an even greater hero. Long after his death he was celebrated in ballads as "Sweet England's Pride" and "the valiant Knight of Chivalry."[3] In *The Rites of Knighthood* I want to analyze the more contentious aspects of Elizabethan chivalry, focusing on the careers of the Earl of Essex, Sir Philip Sidney, and the Earl of Leicester rather than more docile courtiers like Sir Henry Lee. Lee was the Queen's champion for many years and the principal organizer of the Accession Day tilts, and his importance for Elizabethan chivalry has been clearly established by Frances Yates and Roy Strong.[4] Yet Leicester, Sidney, and Essex played equally prominent roles in the court's chivalric spectacles, and their political ambitions were greater and more disruptive than Lee's. They joined in "the rites of knighthood" to assert their own rights and interests, and they made the tilts and tournaments of Elizabeth's court into symbolic power struggles rather than rituals of devotion.

From this perspective the conflicts and the energies at work in Elizabethan chivalry become clearer. Its ceremonial forms constitute a kind of cultural resolution of one of the central contradictions of Elizabethan politics, the conflict between honor and obedience, the "customary rights" of knighthood and the duty to "right royal majesty." Through its conventions of feudal loyalty and romantic devotion, Elizabethan chivalry affirmed Tudor sovereignty. At the same time, it glorified aristocratic militarism and traditional notions of honor and autonomy. The chivalric ideology thus combined deference and aggression, accommodating these dangerously incompatible, often contradictory impulses within its codes and customs. When chivalric rituals worked, they allowed a compromise between the conflicting interests of the Elizabethan ruling class; this capacity to satisfy both crown and nobility explains the enduring popularity of chivalry in the sixteenth century.

Nevertheless, this ceremonial balance of power was often strained by emergent notions of the privileged subject's rights, and the "rites of knighthood" eventually failed to maintain a compromise solution. As in *Richard II*, ritual combat finally could not contain conflicts that were irreconcilable. The chivalric compromise worked for the Earl of Leicester, but Sidney's insistence on his "native and legal freedom" exposed the contradictions of the chivalric code.[5] Even more challenging were the aspirations of the Earl of Essex, who sought to establish the ancient privileges of the Earl Marshal as a basis of independent authority. The historical researches he initiated in 1597 were continued by historians and antiquaries through the seventeenth century, supporting complex and provocative views of England's ancient constitution. The documents commissioned by Essex, some of them previously undiscovered or unexamined, reveal links between the seventeenth-century constitutional theories and earlier ideas of knighthood's "customary rights." Thus, even while they fail to contain or reconcile the conflicts of that time, the political texts of Elizabethan chivalry anticipate some of the ideological shifts of the next age, formulating the rights of the privileged subject against the crown.

My final subject is the chivalric literature that flourished during the reign of Queen Elizabeth, texts ranging from the occasional verse of George Peel to the epic poetry of Edmund Spenser. Many of the texts I shall examine are firmly embedded in cultural practices and bound by social circumstances because they were composed for courtly performance: George Gascoigne's masque of Zabeta along with the antics he improvised for the Earl of Leicester's extravagant show at Kenilworth in 1575, the florid tributes of the Four Foster Children of Desire devised for a tournament in 1581, and the Accession Day device written by Francis Bacon for the Earl of Essex in 1595 were all largely subordinated to their patrons' larger designs. These compositions clearly serve the ceremonial function I ascribe to other events of Elizabethan chivalry since they were often explicitly devised to mediate conflicting interests within the ruling class. Kenneth Burke's concept of symbolic action, so useful to anthropologists and literary critics alike, fits these performances perfectly since it grasps their combination of expressive, ritual, and social functions. As symbolic actions, Elizabethan tournaments and pageants resemble the Balinese cock fights described by Clifford Geertz because they allow a cathartic "expression of open and direct interpersonal and intergroup aggression" without the dangerous consequences of actual combat. At the same time, they serve the purpose assigned to symbolic action by Fredric Jameson, who asserts that "the will to read literary or cultural texts as symbolic acts must necessarily grasp them as resolutions of determinate contradictions." Nevertheless, as we shall see, the conflicts these cultural texts sought to resolve frequently overwhelmed them, disrupting their conciliatory designs and happy endings.[6]

I also examine more purely literary texts, written at a greater distance from courtly performance and the urgent intensity of its conflicts. My last two chapters focus more closely on the careers and major works of two representative writers drawn to chivalric themes and heroes: Samuel Daniel and Edmund Spenser. Each man is also linked through ties of patronage to the historical figures I discuss in the earlier chapters, and both poets celebrate their patrons' chivalric heroism in their verse. Daniel's *Civil Wars* is an ambitious historical poem describing the struggle between crown and nobility in fifteenth-century England. Here too the comparable struggle of his own day encroaches on his work, forcing him to remove verses praising the Earl of Essex from editions published after the Earl's revolt.

Far more pervasive are the effects of Daniel's own ideological confusion, suffusing his verse with fretful inconsistencies and preventing him from bringing his prolonged project to completion. By contrast, Edmund Spenser's verse addresses many of the contradictions of Elizabethan chivalry more obliquely. His greatest work, *The Faerie Queene*, is also unfinished, but its ending is not haunted by the sense of failure that marks *The Civil Wars*, nor does it simply break off. Finally, though Spenser's verse does not reconcile or contain the contradictions it confronts, it manages to comprehend and accept them with greater equanimity. It is thus one of the most successful symbolic actions of Elizabethan chivalry.

Spenser's success derives in part from his belief in the power of poetry, a power Daniel doubts and denies. Daniel declares at the beginning of *The Civil Wars*, "I versifie the troth; not Poetize," and he contends that history's "acted mischiefes" cannot be "unwrought" by poetry's "imagined good." Daniel's verse becomes, in Sir Philip Sidney's terms, a "serving science," subordinate to history and ultimately overwhelmed by its contradictions. For Edmund Spenser, poetry is the supreme vocation, and the poet moves beyond the mere "historiographer." While he does not escape from history altogether, his creation of an "historical fiction" protects his work from the pressures of "present time," allowing a more detached and lucid perspective.[7]

Shakespeare achieves a similar perspective through his own quite different artistic strategies. As we have seen, the Essex revolt encroached on *Richard II*, and Shakespeare praised the Earl in *Henry V* in a speech written after the latter's departure for Ireland, which anticipates a triumphant return:

> Were now the general of our gracious Empress,
> As in good time he may, from Ireland coming,
> Bringing rebellion broached on his sword,
> How many would the peaceful city quit,
> To welcome him!
>
> (*Henry V* V.Ch. 30–34)

Instead of returning with "rebellion broached on his sword," Essex came back to sow rebellion himself, using one of Shakespeare's plays to do so. These events could have proved as discomfiting to Shakespeare as they were for Daniel, but apart from the suppression of the deposition scene in *Richard II*, an act of censorship that preceded the revolt, neither the play nor the playwright was apparently much affected. Instead, far from being overwhelmed by the conflicts they depict, Shakespeare's histories comprehend them by placing them in a diminished but clear perspective. For all his apologetic humility about his "unworthy scaffold" (Pr. 10), Shakespeare pursues his account of Henry V's triumphs to their less glorious conclusion in the epilogue. There the Chorus, "in little room confining mighty men" (Epi. 3), announces the eventual defeat of the king's dynastic and military achievements. The Chorus's equivocal apology for confining and "mangling ... the full course of their glory" (Epi. 4) subtly deflates Henry's triumphant boast that he "cannot be confin'd within the weak list of a country's fashion" (V.ii. 269–270).

Shakespeare's stage, like Spenser's Faery Land, sustains a kind of utopian displacement, its distance from the pressures of immediate controversy allowing a more detached perspective on its social situation. Through such means the literature of Elizabethan chivalry becomes a valuable ideological resource, a useful tool for confronting and comprehending the intractable struggles of the age. Literature of this sort is aptly described, in Kenneth Burke's phrase, as "equipment for living."[8] As Burke explains, the writer who works this way can "fight on his own terms, developing a strategy for imposing the proper 'time, place and conditions.'"[9] A canny command of the terms of engagement is certainly a major component of both Spenser's and Shakespeare's artistic authority. Their authority is not absolute, but even when practical mastery fails, the intellectual mastery their poetry sustains proves valuable. As Burke explains, a writer can challenge a system even as he seems to submit to it, since he "confronts contradictions. Insofar as they are resolvable contradictions he acts to resolve them. Insofar as they are not resolvable, he symbolically erects a 'higher synthesis' in poetic and conceptual imagery that helps him to 'accept' them."[10] Burke's bracketed and ironic notion of "acceptance" resembles Stephen Greenblatt's concept of "subversive submission" articulated in *Renaissance Self-Fashioning*, but Burke's "acceptance" is less easily contained.[11] Since, according to Burke, its poetic syntheses "name both friendly and unfriendly forces, they fix attitudes that prepare for combat."[12]

Burke's pragmatic and combative notion of poetry as a valuable ideological tool is as important to my understanding of the literature of Elizabethan chivalry as his concept of symbolic action; so too is his emphasis on the intellectual freedom that poetry allows. This emphasis has been noted and criticized by others who have drawn on his thinking. Fredric Jameson says that Burke's "too immediate celebration of the free creativity of human language (in its broadest sense) overleaps the whole dimension of our (nonnatural) determination by transindividual historical forces."[13] Historical determinism is certainly the fashion in much current criticism, but it has become too grimly categorical in its nullification of all individual autonomy. Jonathan Goldberg declares that "to live the poet's life means to surrender to an other, authoring swallowed in authority.... Power encompasses and straitens poetic production, producing the poet and 'his' text."[14] The writer's authority collapses often enough before the hegemony of political power in many of the texts and performances I discuss, but claims such as Goldberg's are finally too undiscriminating. In my view, a belief in a greater degree of creative intellectual independence for some writers is justified by much of the political thought and literature of late Elizabethan England since several of the texts I examine anticipate the challenges to sovereign authority enacted in the Civil War: in Burke's terms, "they fix attitudes that prepare for combat."

Much of the value of Elizabethan chivalry for English political thought derives from its legitimation of combativeness itself. This pugnacity combined with an affirmation of the "customary rights" of privileged subjects to keep alive fundamental principles of freedom and dissent throughout the sixteenth century. On its own, Elizabethan chivalry failed to realize these ideals in practice, as the careers of Leicester, Sidney, and Essex clearly demonstrate. Yet chivalry, in consort with other radical movements, constituted a significant ideological challenge. J. E. Neale has noted the important contribution of Puritanism to "the art of opposition" in Elizabethan parliaments.[15] Puritan clergymen also turned up at Essex House on the eve of the revolt to preach the right of the noble magnate to lead opposition to tyranny. This inchoate alliance between aristocratic chivalry and Protestant zeal failed in 1601, but, as I shall suggest in my conclusion, it succeeded in the opening stages of the Civil War. Moreover, its success in practice was anticipated in theory by one of the great works of Elizabethan chivalric fiction. For John Milton, among others, Spenser's *Faerie Queene* fully realized an ideal synthesis of religious fervor and chivalric honor. By celebrating a "true warfaring Christian" who may also be "wayfaring," Spenser helped Milton and other readers to prepare for both political and spiritual combat.[16]

1

Chivalric Compromise and Conflict

In England in the sixteenth century a crucial power shift occurred. In his dedication to *The Collection of the History of England* Samuel Daniel looked back over the regime of the "fiue Soueraigne Princes of the line of Tewdor" with a certain rueful ambivalence, describing it as "a time not of that virilitie as the former, but more subtile, and let out into wider notions, and bolder discoveries of what lay hidden before. A time wherein began a greater improvement of the Soueraigntie, and more came to be effected by wit then by the sword." Daniel's dismay at the diminished "virilitie" of his own age was widely shared and further aggravated, under Elizabeth, by subordination to a female ruler. The reign of James with its courtly corruption and appeasement of Spain only increased these anxieties. Daniel offers a poignant contemporary account of what Lawrence Stone has called the "crisis of the aristocracy," a crisis in which the crown gradually gained ascendancy over its once overmighty subjects.[1]

Nevertheless, royal dominion was not absolute, and the nobility retained much of their power and even more of their prestige, while their pride was undiminished. The monarchy still depended on them to raise troops, and their predilection for warfare and violence continued unabated.[2] Indeed, war remained the supreme vocation for many noblemen, who regard it as an opportunity for winning honor and renown. "Despite the rival claims of administration, government and letters, it was still the duty of a true nobleman to follow the profession of arms" throughout the Renaissance, according to Malcolm Vale.[3] Elizabeth's court swarmed with unruly men of the sword, who rushed off to do battle in the Netherlands, Ireland, and the New World.

The enthusiasm of the nobility for war created a split within the ruling class, one that Sir Robert Naunton describes in his memoirs of the period, *Fragmenta Regalia*. Naunton divides Elizabeth's court into two factions, the *militia* and the *togati*, roughly analogous to the *noblesse d'épée* and the *noblesse de robe* in France.[4] He imputes a certain ambivalence to the Queen regarding her *militia*, contending that "she loved a soldier" while acknowledging that their "absence and their many eruptions were very distasteful unto her" (p. 56). Certainly their reckless bravado and blustering arrogance often sorely tried her patience. Typical of Naunton's *militia* is Sir John Perrot, his wife's grandfather and a bluff soldier whose irascible temper landed him in the Tower, where he died in 1592.

In 1571 Perrot commanded the English forces in Munster. Frustrated by his inability to force a decisive engagement with the Irish rebels, he made an extraordinary move, challenging their leader, James Fitzmaurice, to single combat, "to make an end of this war" with one blow. Fitzmaurice haggled over the terms of combat for some time, initially proposing "sword and target and Irish trousers" for both men, then fifty men on each side, and finally twelve on horseback and twelve on foot "with indifferent armour and weapon." After stringing Perrot along and extracting his agreement to each proposal, Fitzmaurice finally failed to arrive at the appointed time and place, sending a message instead that sensibly explained that "if I should kill Sir John Perrot, the Queen of England can send another President unto this province; but if he do kill me, there is none other to succeed me, or to command as I do, therefore I will not willingly fight with him." Perrot was embarrassed by his enemy's escape on this occasion, but the English general eventually flushed "the fox out of his hole" and then triumphed, forcing the rebellious Fitzmaurice to surrender on bended knee at sword's point a year later.[5] Perrot was subsequently appointed Lord Deputy of Ireland in 1584, replacing Lord Grey de Wilton, who had been recalled in 1582.

Perrot was less fortunate at court, where according to Naunton his "desire to be in command at home as he had been abroad" embroiled him in grave difficulties (Naunton, p. 66).

His enemies accused him of treason, and although the Queen dismissed these accusations for a time, Perrot's irrepressible temper gave rise to further charges. When he surmised she would request his aid against the invasion of the Armada, he boasted that "now she is ready to bepiss herself for fear of the Spaniard, I am again one of her white boys" (p. 67). Charged with speaking contemptuous words against the Queen, he was arrested in 1591. Perrot was undaunted by his arrest or by the dire prospect of a treason trial, for "at his arraignment he was so little dejected" that "he despised his jury, though of the order of knighthood and of the especial gentry, claiming the privilege of trial by the peers and baronage of the realm." In Naunton's view, it was Perrot's "haughtiness of spirit" that finally killed him since "it broke in pieces the cords of his magnanimity" when "he died suddenly in the Tower" in 1592 (p. 67).

Naunton tells Perrot's story as a cautionary tale that provides "instructions to persons in place of honor and command to beware of the violences of nature" (Naunton, p. 67). Perrot was a man who "loved to stand too much alone and on his own legs, and of too often recesses and discontinuance from the Queen's presence, a fault which is incompatible with the ways of the court and favor" (p. 65). It was a mistake Naunton himself would never make. As a young man, Naunton fell briefly under the sway of the most reckless of Elizabeth's *militia*, the Earl of Essex, entering into his service as a spy in France in 1596. Loathing such employment and perhaps sensing the dangers of service to the Earl, Naunton withdrew in 1599 to the safe haven of Cambridge, where he became university orator and proctor, escaping the smashup of Essex and his faction.[6] By 1602 he returned to court and aligned himself with Robert Cecil, whose triumph was assured by Essex's defeat. Naunton prospered under James, rising to become Secretary of State in 1618 with the assistance of the King's favorite, the Duke of Buckingham. Naunton fell from favor and high office for a time near the end of James's reign, but he quickly recovered, retaining his seat on the Privy Council and a lucrative sinecure under Charles until his death in 1635.[7] In his own career

Naunton emulated one of the greatest success stories of his memoir, that of William Paulet, Marquess of Winchester, a man who survived the reigns of four Tudor monarchs from Henry VIII through Elizabeth. He was asked "how he stood for thirty years together amidst the changes and ruins of so many counselors and great personalities. 'Why' quoth the Marquess, '*ortus sum ex salice non ex quercu*. I was made of the pliable willow, not of the oak'" (pp. 47–48).

Such pliancy served many courtiers quite well, but Elizabeth's *militia* found it hard to submit to its requirements. One of the latter group's staunchest members, Lord Willoughby de Eresby, insisted that "he was none of the *reptilia*, intimating that he could not creep and crouch. Neither was the court his element, for indeed as he was a great soldier, so was he of a suitable magnanimity and could not brook the obsequiousness and assiduity of the court" (Naunton, pp. 61–62). Willoughby's boasts show how readily the defiant belligerence of the *militia* could easily degenerate into the reckless arrogance of the *miles gloriosus*. Nevertheless, the virtue he embraces was still regarded as the quintessence of nobility in the Renaissance, and it was still inextricably linked with the career of "a great soldier." Magnanimity or "greatness of soul" is classically sanctioned in Aristotle's *Nicomachean Ethics*, and it came to mean "a certaine excellencie of courage, which aiming at honour, directeth all his doings therevnto, and specially vnto vertue."[8] Its close connection with courage makes honor an essentially military virtue, rooted in Roman *virtu*, and it became the greatest good, "valued aboue all earthly wealth."[9]

The aristocratic code of honor presents several ethical and political problems. Its inherent moral inconsistency is evident in Aristotle, who says that although the magnanimous man must be honored, he cannot "live in dependence upon somebody else." At the same time, "honour is felt to depend more on those who confer than on him who receives it."[10] The main question is thus who confers it and why. Throughout the Renaissance most agree that only the monarch can do so. Francis Markham writes, "But in whose keeping is this inestimable Iewell? Is so sacred a thing fit for a mortall disposition? Is man the master of so rich Treasure? Yes, he is; yet but the King only."[11] The traditional notion of the monarchy as "the fountaine of all Nobilitie" is repeatedly invoked by the Elizabethan herald, Robert Glover, in *The Catalogue of Honor*, and his nephew, Thomas Milles, adds in his "Peroration" to that work that kings are "the moderators of the vertuous endeuors, and onely Creators of all Titles of Honour."[12]

Glover complicates matters by distinguishing between moral and political nobility and breaking the latter into two subcategories, "native" and "dative" titles of honor.[13] He tries to finesse the problems raised by his own distinctions by emphasizing the monarch's control over both: "native" honors are also the king's gift, according to Glover, but kings "gouerne Nobility according to their owne pleasure and good like, and so, haue made the same heraeditary."[14] However, hereditary honors, such as peerages, come to be seen as inalienable and even "indelible." The "character *indelebilis*" of the title baron was asserted in a trial held in the Court of Chivalry in 1597.[15] "Native" nobility creates a belief in inherent moral and ancestral distinction, and this assumption is in turn linked to the aristocracy's sense of its "customary rights" and privileges, rights that a monarch like Richard II denies at his peril. Like many writers on the subject of honor, Glover is dimly aware of its contradictions and tries to gloss them over with sophistical double-talk: "But Customes are still like themselues, neither are wee to detract from the authority of Kinges, who although they haue such supereminent, and vndeterminate prerogatiue, as that they may seeme somtime to haue of fauour graunted, some thinges beside the Lawes; yet shall it not appeare them requested, to haue requested, to haue done, or yet suffered any thing to bee done, contrary vnto the Customes of Stockes & Families."[16] Thus, the king's "supereminent, and vndeterminate prerogatiue" is still bound by a belief in the "customary rights" of noble families.

The ideal of aristocratic honor thus created a sense of aggressive independence and authority that posed serious political problems. As Mervyn James has shown in his study of the subject, the concept of honor was at the heart of one of the central contradictions of Elizabethan politics: the conflict between aristocratic self-esteem and autonomy and the demands of obedience and duty to the monarch.[17] For men like Naunton, self-interest had to be accommodated to the sovereign's demands. However, for many members of the *militia*, such pliancy was too demeaning because Naunton's assiduous docility conflicted with the code of honor. Some outlet for aristocratic pride and magnanimity was required.

For a great many aristocrats, Elizabethan chivalry provided such an outlet. The revival of "the rites of knighthood" kept alive the aristocracy's sense of their "customary rights." What Malcolm Vale says of fifteenth-century chivalry remains true for the Elizabethan period as well: "In the achievement of honour, prowess and renown, the tournament still held a central and unchallenged place."[18] The bellicose Sir John Perrot prided himself on his skill in the tiltyard. Under Edward he "gayned a speciall Reputation [by] Expertness in Actes of Chivalry, as Tylte, Turney, Bariers, and the lyke, wherein he did exercise and shew hymselfe," and he appeared in several tournaments at the beginning of Elizabeth's reign.[19] Characteristically, he was one of the most aggressive contestants in Elizabeth's coronation tournament, where he "hit the challenger four tymes on the face of the healm with the pommell of his sword," scoring more blows of this sort than any of the other defendants. In a tournament the next year Perrot broke more staves than anyone else.[20] Finally, in a tournament incongruously staged to entertain the French ambassador in July of 1559, Perrot and his opponent became angry with one another after the other rider and his horse were injured by Perrot's lance. They had already been fighting without a tilt when they began charging one another "with sharpe Launces without Armour in the Presence of the Queene."[21] Elizabeth swiftly intervened, forcing them to stop; the French ambassador, whose King had just died from injuries sustained in a tilting accident, excused himself from the banquet afterward, saying that "all Shewes and Intertaynmentes sounded nothing but Sorow into his Eares and Senses."[22]

Elizabeth's reign fostered a spectacular revival of chivalric ideals and practices. Her Accession Day and other state occasions were solemnly celebrated with tournaments and chivalric pageants. They combined ceremonial devotion and formality with sporadic outbursts of unruly belligerence. Many of them were commemorated by poets and writers of the period, and Sir Philip Sidney's *Arcadia* and Edmund Spenser's *Faerie Queene* are thought to have drawn inspiration from "the living springs in living pageantry" of Elizabethan chivalry.[23] At the same time, "the rites of knighthood" were strikingly dramatized in the plays of Shakespeare, Marlowe, Peele, and many others. Life in turn tended to imitate art as various aristocratic warriors performed deeds in battle that were both grandly heroic and literally quixotic. Their chivalric gallantry and courage were supposedly the highest form of loyal service, but more often than not, their heroics put them at odds with their Queen. The vagaries and contradictions of Elizabethan chivalry are quite perplexing, and they have prompted a number of opposing historical explanations.

Many historians feel that the spectacles, fictions, and exploits of Elizabethan chivalry are sustained by mere delusions. The entire chivalric revival is seen as a nostalgic anachronism and escapist fantasy of a decadent ruling class. Anthony Esler dismisses the chivalric ideals of men like Essex and Sidney with a contempt that is breathtakingly supercilious: "All these Elizabethans had a remarkable facility for swathing and muffling facts in pink clouds of fiction. They clothed their lives in lovely little Arabian Nights's entertainments which served to soften the rough edge of reality whenever it forced itself upon the consciousness." Arthur Ferguson is less patronizing and more informative, but he still regards chivalry as a merely personal and "patently outdated code of values" that "has lost any necessary connection with the life of the gentleman considered as a functioning member of the body politic." His more recent book speaks of chivalry's "continued vitality" in the sixteenth century, but his perspective is unchanged. Ferguson still believes that "power was a concept alien to the chivalric idea" and that its "sources were more romantic than sociological." Behind such thinking is a traditional view of chivalry that considers it, in the words of William Schofield, "less an institution than an ideal" in which "the spirit wars against the flesh, the idea against the fact, in the lives of nations as well as individuals."[24]

Other historians recognize the enduring political significance of Elizabethan chivalry, but they see it as the ceremonial and ideological monopoly of Tudor sovereignty. Frances Yates contends that it was used to focus "fervent religious loyalty on the national monarch." Roy Strong maintains that "the imagery and motifs of legends of chivalry formed an integral part of the official 'image' projected by sixteenth century monarchs."[25] In his earlier work on the chivalric pageantry of the Tudor, Valois, and Hapsburg courts, Strong contends that Renaissance tournaments became "a predetermined saga" whose "feudal realities" faded away; through these elaborately organized spectacles "the truths of a sacred monarchy could be propagated to the court and a tamed nobility take its place in the round of ritual."[26]

A more complete understanding of Elizabethan chivalry must recognize both its full political importance and its enduring aristocratic bias. As its etymology indicates, chivalry, from the French *chevalrie*, originally meant skill on horseback, an accomplishment only the well-born could afford. It began as an early medieval warrior code, whose essential values were strength, conquest, and renown. In the twelfth century, its supposedly classical apex, chivalry acquired a religious justification with the organization of the Crusades, and it became aligned with ideas of courtly love and service. Yet despite these mollifying influences, chivalry's essential purpose was to justify aristocratic authority and warmongering. Ramon Lull's definitive text, *Libre del Ordre de Cavayleria*, written in the thirteenth century and widely circulated and translated through the fifteenth century, makes this clear. Originally incorporated into feudalism, chivalry is a system of "power and dominacion" in which knights rule "ouer the moyen [middle] peple" as kings ruled over them. Domination is partially softened by an obligation to assist the weak: "Thoffyce of a knyght is to mayntene

and deffende wymmen wydowes and orphanes and men dys-
eased an not puyssaunt ne stronge. For lyke as cust018me and
reason is that the grettest and moost myghty helpe the feble
and lasse and that they haue recours to the grete. Ryght soo is
thordre of chyualry." Nevertheless, these more compassionate
impulses do not alter the commitment to force and control. As
Lull says elsewhere, "Thoffyce of a knyght is to mayntene the
londe for by cause that the drede of the comyn people haue of
the knyghtes they laboure and cultyue the erthe for fere leste
they shold be destroyed." He complacently adds that "in
seygnorye is moche noblesse & in seruytude as moche of
subiections."[27]

Chivalry survived the demise of feudalism in the late middle
ages because the aristocracy retained their authority as well as
their military ambitions. J. E. A. Jollife describes the development during the fourteenth century of "a new chivalry, more
exacting than the old and calling forth loyalties which cut
across the remaining feudal ties" and in which military service
was still the essential element.[28] The English aristocracy became, if anything, even more actively bellicose during the
fifteenth-century Wars of the Roses, but, at the same time,
chivalric spectacle and literature grew more elaborate and
romantic under the influence of Burgundian pageantry. In his
study of Malory's *Morte Darthur* Larry Benson shows the ideological value of chivalric romance to the nobility in its
"insistence upon those qualities that set them apart as a class
and … an emphasis on an ideal of noble conduct that defined
that class."[29]

Maurice Keen's magisterial study, *Chivalry*, provides the
most accurate and complete account of the long history of
chivalry from its early to late stages. In his view, later develop-
ments led to neither decadent nostalgia nor the dominance of
the monarchy. Instead, chivalry evolved by the fifteenth century into an "unwritten compromise between government and
nobility," in which the crown acquiesced to "the maintenance
of noble social dominance and noble privilege" as well as "the
martial aspirations of nobility."[30] According to Malcolm Vale,

such a compromise was still necessary even in the sixteenth century because "the crown could not afford to alienate a bellicose nobility by withholding what they considered an inalienable right to submit disputes to the test of skill-at-arms in single combat. If warfare offered fewer opportunities of testing that skill, the duel at least provided a substitute." With the growing reliance on siege tactics, mercenary soldiers, and modern ballistics, the terms and conditions of battle changed, and the chivalric code "entered a phase of decay from which it never recovered," in Vale's view. Yet he insists on the continuity between "the medieval cult of chivalry" and the "Renaissance cult of honour" that replaces it, since the latter was just as defiantly bellicose.[31] Moreover, even if sixteenth-century warfare proved less congenial to chivalric exploits, many English aristocrats still resorted to it anyway to vindicate their honor and authority. Despite the altered nature of battle, the links between war and chivalry persisted. Keen also succumbs to vague cliches about chivalry's exhaustion and "a lack of genuinely new departures" in the sixteenth century to justify stopping his survey with the year 1500, but his charges are confusing. Since Elizabethan chivalry was deliberately archaic, little value was attached to innovation. Moreover, its literature and spectacles were certainly as creatively vigorous as anything in fifteenth-century England. Keen concludes more accurately that chivalry underwent a "change, rather than a decline" in its values and customs. "The chivalric concept of nobility lost none of its force, and the notions of its essential constituents—loyalty, generosity and courage—were not much altered. Where old ways, modified as necessary, could be related to altered structures, there chivalry did not fade or decline with the coming of the Renaissance."[32]

Elizabethan chivalry was thus a continuing compromise between the Queen and her fractious aristocrats, one in which she had the upper hand but still conceded a great deal. The chivalric ceremonies and institutions of her court were as much a celebration of the aristocracy's enduring "martial aspirations" and exalted social status as they were a tribute to Elizabeth. The Queen did not mind sharing the ceremonial stage with her nobility, allowing them to move through the city and the court in what Wallace MacCaffrey calls "an atmosphere of almost reverential respect."[33] She immediately grasped what Francis Bacon spells out in his essay "Of Nobility": "Nobility attempers Soveraignty, and drawes the Eyes of the People, somewhat aside from the Line Royall."[34] Nevertheless, Elizabeth tolerated and even encouraged this state of affairs, letting her noble luminaries shine as long as they did not threaten to eclipse her. She permitted Thomas Howard, the Duke of Norfolk, "to retain a hundred men in his service, ...notwithstanding the Act against Retainers," and he was escorted to and from London by a "worthy company," making his passage through the city into a kind of formal progress.[35] She permitted Leicester, Cecil, and Shrewsbury to do the same. As J. E. Neale points out, a magnate's entourage constituted "a minor court within the Court proper. The world saw his greatness reflected therein."[36]

The Order of the Garter institutionalized this chivalric compromise. The value of the Order in securing loyalty to the crown has frequently been noted, but it was also important as a showcase for noble grandeur.[37] The size and magnificence of the retinue attending upon the knights at their induction swelled to such an extent that James I took steps to suppress such excesses, but the custom persisted after his death.[38] In 1629 the Earl of Northampton rode "with such splendour and gallantry and exhibited so brilliant a cortege, being attended by nearly a hundred persons, that a vote of thanks was decreed to him by the Chapter of the Order."[39] Elizabeth was less anxious about sharing the stage with her nobility, an aspect of her style Roy Strong perceptively emphasizes in contrasting it with the increasingly absolutist esthetic of the Stuart court:

> The new premises were promoted by a new dynasty, who saw the lines of geometrical totality converging upon themselves, exalting their divinity to new heights of grandeur. Elizabeth had no need for such lines of false perspective to draw men's eyes to contemplate her. The basic assumption of Elizabethan vision suited her well, above all because it was more comprehensive, diffuse, and ambiguous. The strength of the

Elizabethan image lay in its capacity to be read and reread many ways and never to present a single outright statement which left no room for manoeuvre, as did its successors in the new style.[40]

For a monarch less intent on ceremonial autocracy, the Order of the Garter allowed a more balanced relationship. Fraternal fellowship, rather than hierarchy, was the organizing principle. John Ferne, writing in 1586, says that the annual feast was held by the members at Windsor Castle for the sake of honor and the nation's fame and "also to novrish vp loue and amity amongst them."[41] Amity is indeed one of the principal social functions of the institution. Edward VI's revised charter declares that the Order's purpose is twofold: "to aduance to honor and glory good, godly, valiant, well couraged, wise and noble men for their notable desertes, and to nourishe a certaine amytie, fellowship, and agrement in all honest thinges among all men, but specially among equalles in degre, for they do iudge honor, as surely it is, the rewarde of vertue, and concorde the fundation and enlarger of common weales."[42] In his "Peroration" to the *Catalogue of Honor* Thomas Milles sees the Order as a utopian institution joining the aristocracy and the monarchy as well as native and dative honor in a mystical union:

> For heere, All behold MAIESTY her selfe, between GREATNESSE and DECORVM, descend from her Throne, to walke and talke kindly with hir owne Nobility: and NOBILITY it selfe between HONOR and REVERENCE, accending on the Seat of her owne SOVERAIGNE MAIESTY ...
>
> And heere our KING with his PRINCE, our PRINCE with his PEERS, and our PEERS with their WORTHIES, meete and march together in one Bond of Loue, in one Order of Chiualry, for mutuall Defence both of Church and Commonwealth, amazing the Beholders with the stately sight & view of ONE personall MAIESTY, in ONE Fellowship of HONOR, and ONE BODY of vnstained and true NOBILITY.[43]

The Order of the Garter thus reconciles and accommodates the conflicting demands of honor and duty, allowing majesty to descend and nobility to ascend to "meete and marche together in one Bond of Loue, in one Order of Chivalry."

For Elizabethan chivalry, the main event was still the tournament, especially the Accession Day tilt, and it combined many
of the splendors of the Garter ceremonies with the thrill of
combat. The contestants entered the tiltyard in a chariot or on
horseback, richly armed and attired and accompanied by a procession of liveried retainers.[44] These entries were an opportunity for extravagant shows of greatness, and they were
often as much a celebration of the contestants' own status and
splendor as a tribute to the Queen. After his first arrest and exclusion from the tiltyard, the Earl of Essex confessed to the
Queen that those who enter and "stand in the bright beams of
your presence, rejoice partly for your Majesty's, but partly for
their own happiness."[45] Indeed, Essex and his cohorts dominated the tiltyard after the retirement of Sir Henry Lee in 1590,
and their motives, as he admits, were less devotional than self-
aggrandizing.

The tilt itself was no less dramatic than the entry. Two
knights on horseback charged along a tilt, or barrier, their reba-
ted lances aimed at each other's helmet or breastplate; points
were awarded for each lance broken. A heraldic illustration
from early in Elizabeth's reign gives some sense of the excitement of such an event (Figure 1).[46] It shows the wall at the
center dividing the two contestants. The knight on the right
scores a hit, or attaint, while his opponent misses. Below the
victorious contestant are the shattered remains of a lance, the
sign of his prowess in a previous course. The heralds and their
assistants briskly officiate while the judges look on from a gallery. Meanwhile the other knights eagerly await their turn,
their horses' hooves stamping the earth. The picture is one of
several illustrating John Tiptoft's fifteenth-century ordinances
for "Justes of Peace Royall," rules that Sir John Harington contends were officially revived in 1562.[47] Tiptoft gives the most
points for hits that are difficult or dangerous—blows to the
helmet, blows that unseat the opponent, and blows on the
lance's tip, or "coronall to coronall."[48]

During the course of Elizabeth's reign, Tiptoft's distinctions
lost their point as steps were taken to insure that the competition remained friendly. Tournaments became safer and less
aggressive as lances were made "increasingly fragile" and con-

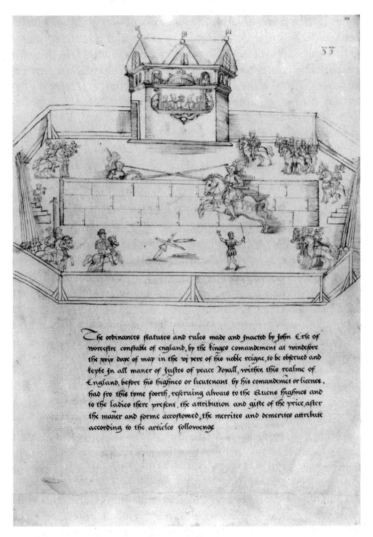

The ordinances statutes and rules made and inacted by John Erle of
worcestre constable of england, by the kinges comandement at windesore
the xxix daye of may in the vj yere of his noble reigne, to be obserued and
kepte in all maner of justes of peace Royall, within this realme of
England, before his highnes or lieutenant by his comandement or licence,
had fro this tyme foorth, reseruing alwaie to the Quene highnes and
to the ladies there present, the attribution and gifte of the price after
the maner and forme accostomed, the merrites and demerites attribute
according to the articles followenge

1. Tilt with lances (College of Arms, MS M6, reproduced by permission of the College of Arms).

testants aimed for the chest instead of the head.[49] Earlier in the century, in 1559, Henri II of France had been killed when a splintered lance penetrated his visor and pierced his brain, and Henry VIII narrowly escaped a similar fatal injury. Such accidents were avoided by these increased safety measures. Moreover, the later Elizabethan tournaments seemed designed to spare their participants from humiliation as well as harm. As Sydney Anglo notes, the heralds stopped keeping score, declaring instead that everybody "did well": "There was, apparently, an ancient chivalric convention which forbade the heralds, in their proclamation, from informing the assembled ladies just how miserably their knights had performed."[50] The same tendency is evident in George Peele's verse accounts of the Accession Day tilts. In *Polyhymnia* Peele lists the "names of the Lordes and Gentlemen that ran, and the order of their running" in the 1590 Accession Day tilt without indicating how they did, and his praises remain scrupulously impartial:

> Peace then my muse, yet ere thou peace, report,
> Say how thou sawest these Actors play their partes
> Both mounted bravely, bravelie minded both,
> Second to few or none for their successe;
> Their hie devoyre, ther deed do say no lesse.[51]

In *Anglorum Feriae*, when he describes the performance of the three Knollys brothers in the Accession Day tilt of 1595, he again finds it "harde to say which brother did the best."[52] But between the lines of blandly uniform praise there are occasional hints that not everyone "did well." William Segar was sent to the Netherlands with the Earl of Leicester as Portcullis Pursuivant to record the pomp and spectacle of the latter's triumphal progress. In his account of the combat performed on St. George's Day in Utrecht, Segar writes, "The barriers [were] done, and eyther part retyred with equall prayse (though not with equall blowes)."[53]

Segar's brief reference to unequal blows reminds us that tournaments still consisted of conflict as well as compliment, and aggressive competition as well as stately ceremony. Although no longer the brutal and dangerous war game that it was in the Middle Ages, the Elizabethan tournament was still a strenuous and dynamic event, and like any sporting contest it allowed a release of aggressive energies. Moreover, it was also a symbolic substitute for war. Throughout the Renaissance the aristocracy still regarded battle as an "occasion for honorable self-display and the public performance of 'fine deeds.'"[54] In its combination of ostentation and martial prowess the tournament provided an even more theatrically satisfying opportunity for "honorable self-display" before a much larger audience. As Alan Young says, these events presented a "spectacle of a nation in microcosm."[55] An illustration from the same heraldic document showing combat on foot with swords suggests the size and motley variety of the crowds that flocked to these spectacles, crowds that according to contemporary accounts could number in the thousands (Figure 2).[56] The lame and the tattered poor, as well as children and animals, jostled prosperous citizens and elegant courtiers for a glimpse of "the rites of knighthood."

From one point of view Elizabethan tournaments functioned as a classic safety valve, allowing a socially sanctioned and carefully regulated release of aggressive energies. From this perspective they fulfilled the purpose ascribed to symbolic action by Clifford Geertz; there are certainly several parallels between these chivalric spectacles and the Balinese cockfight he describes. In both contests "prestige, the necessity to affirm it, defend it, celebrate it, justify it, and just plain bask in it ... is perhaps the central driving force." In both, mock combat allows a release of aggression as well as the "sensation of drastic and momentary movement" without any dire consequences. Indeed, they "have had their practical consequences removed and been reduced (or, if you prefer, raised) to the level of sheer appearances, where their meaning can be more powerfully articulated and more exactly perceived."[57] Geertz's concept of "deep play" nicely captures the fundamental instability of such events, something the brother of the Grand Turk notes in Castiglione's *Book of the Courtier*: the foreign observer, "being a captive at Rome, said that jousting, as we practice it in Italy, seemed to him too much if done in play and too little if done in earnest."[58] Yet for Geertz, in the last analysis, sym-

2. Combat with swords (College of Arms, MS M6, reproduced by permission of the College of Arms).

bolic action is largely symbolic and inconsequential, and he invokes W. H. Auden to assert that ritual combat, like poetry, "makes nothing happen."[59]

Geertz's emphasis on the merely symbolic side of symbolic action distorts Burke's original notion of both symbolic action and poetry, which the latter says "is designed to 'do something' for the poet and his readers."[60] Geertz also fails to grasp the complex and unsettling energies of symbolic action and the motives of those involved. Certainly many who joined in "the rites of knighthood" did so in order to make something happen, hoping thereby to reclaim some of the power and glory of the chivalric warrior. Some even saw them as a means of regaining the customary "rights" of knighthood. Such desires are made strikingly, even alarmingly, clear in the *Vindiciae Contra Tyrannos*, a Huguenot tract generally attributed to the aristocrat Philippe de Mornay, a counselor to Henry of Navarre and friend of Sir Philip Sidney.[61] Like other Huguenot treatises, the *Vindiciae* combines an equivocal justification of noble rebellion against tyranny with what Michael Walzer calls "an unsuccessful effort to transform feudal status into constitutional position."[62] The anonymous author of this revolutionary treatise chastens his peers for regarding tournaments and chivalric fetes as empty theatricals:

> Let electors, palatines, peers, and the other notables not assume that they were created and ordained merely to appear at coronations and dress up in splendid uniforms of olden times, as though they were actors in an ancient masque playing the parts of a Roland, Oliver, Renaldo, or any other great hero for a day, or as though they were staging a scene from King Arthur and the Knights of the Round Table as they are called; and that when the crowd has gone and Calliope has said farewell, they have played their parts in full. These ceremonies are not celebrated for amusement; they are not *pro forma*; and they are not the games of children who, like Horace, create imaginary kings. Let the magnates remember, rather, that if the role which they receive brings honor, it carries many burdens also. The commonwealth has no doubt been committed and entrusted to the king as its supreme and principal protector, and yet to them also, as its co-protectors.[63]

From this participant's perspective, tournaments are not prized for their lack of "practical consequences" or honorific symbolism. On the contrary, they are a potent ritual that initiates the participants into the rights and responsibilities of their traditional chivalric role. The contestants are encouraged to enact the role seriously, exercising its military and political authority completely, even if that means opposing sovereign majesty.

Few aristocrats wanted to take their role that far in France or in England. The nobility's own large stake in the status quo dampened their enthusiasm for revolution or radical speculation. Many were in fact quite content to "dress up in splendid uniforms" and play the "great hero for a day." One of the most frequent participants in the later Accession Day tilts was Lord Compton, who ran sixteen times between 1589 and 1602.[64] Aligned with no faction and driven by no strong military ambitions, Compton was apparently motivated by nothing more than a passion for conspicuous consumption—a passion shared by many of his peers. For such men, "the rites of knighthood" had become more or less empty delusions of grandeur.

For a number of others, the ideals and customs of Elizabethan chivalry entailed a more substantial political commitment. Robert Dudley, the Earl of Leicester, eventually settled for the gratifications of "sheer appearances," but for a long time he used chivalric symbolism and spectacle to advance his considerable ambitions against his many enemies at court. He usually came away the victor from these symbolic power struggles and reached something like a draw in his encounters with the Queen. His nephew, Sir Philip Sidney, was less fortunate and often felt more estranged from the pomp and triumphs of the tiltyard. Nevertheless, he continued to participate in the rites of Elizabethan chivalry while commemorating his deeds and devices there in verse and prose. His legendary death in battle fixed his identity as a chivalric martyr. Finally, the Earl of Essex was a prominent contestant in the Accession Day tilts and a courageous and popular warrior who followed the exhortations of the *Vindiciae* to their logical conclusion and rose in rebellion against his monarch. Each of these men turned to "the rites of knighthood" to assert his own rights and ambitions. Their aggressive energies invigorated the ritualized combat of Elizabethan chivalry even as they strained the chivalric compromise to its breaking point. These men also inspired the imaginations of the poets who celebrated their ideals. As we shall see in our analysis of the careers of Leicester, Sidney, and Essex, in their chivalric spectacles something always happened.

2

Robert Dudley:
"Favour Sufficient"

For the Christmas season of 1524 a sumptuous but sturdy structure was erected in the tiltyard at Greenwich, which was called the Castle of Loyalty. Participants indicated their choice of arms and the type of combat by touching one of the four colored shields held by a large unicorn placed in front of the castle (Figure 3).[1] This tournament was only one of a series of extravagant chivalric spectacles staged by Henry VIII. The main event was an assault on the castle, and this turned out to be an especially rough affair. After the first day's siege, several challengers concluded that "the Castel could not be wonne by sport, but [only] by ernest," and so "soddainely all the young persones without, threw stones at them within the castle, and they at theim, and many honest men which threw not wer hurt, and with much pein thei without wer apeised, and no man knew how nor why, this hurlyng began."[2] Early Tudor tournaments were designed to glorify the monarch's prowess and magnificence, but they were hardly carefully stage-managed events. They retained much of the boisterous energy and belligerence of medieval melee.[3] Indeed, Henry himself was nearly killed in a tournament earlier the same year when he left his visor open and the Duke of Suffolk's lance splintered inside his helmet. The King's appearance in the lists of the Castle of Loyalty seems to have been designed to dispel fears of mortality aroused by that near miss. Henry and his opponent, once again the Duke of Suffolk, entered disguised as "ancient knightes, with beardes of silver," proclaiming to the Queen and her ladies "that although youth had left them, and age was come, and would lette [hinder] theim to do feactes of armes:

3. Castle of Loyalty (College of Arms, MS M6, reproduced by permission of the College of Arms).

Yet courage, desire, and good will abode with theim, and bad theim to take vpon theim to breake speres." When the ladies gave their consent, the two men threw off their disguises and did combat with great vigor, according to Hall, who says that the spectators "preised and marveiled at the kynges strength, for thei saw his speres were broken with more force then the other speres wer."[4] However, despite this brave show, the Castle of Loyalty marked a turning point in Henry's chivalric career, for it was essentially his "last major tournament."[5] He did not participate in the next tilt, in February 1526, one that was again marred by an accident with a shattered spear; this time the victim, Sir Francis Brian, lost an eye.[6] From that point on, Henry's zeal for tournaments diminished as his age, girth, and debts increased.[7]

For another participant, the Castle of Loyalty was a more positive turning point. It marked the first recorded appearance in the lists of John Dudley, signaling an upturn in his personal fortunes. He was the son of Edmund Dudley, the hated but invaluable minister of Henry VII. Henry VIII had executed the elder Dudley and Richard Empson at the beginning of his reign, sacrificing his father's aides to the wrath of their many enemies; but John was restored in blood in 1513 and his father's attainder lifted. John began to prosper once his chivalric and military skills brought him to his monarch's attention. He joined the Duke of Suffolk in Calais, and the Duke knighted him there. The next year he joined the combat at the Castle of Loyalty. A capable and courageous commander in several campaigns, he thrived as a military officer under Henry and then Edward, acquiring several posts, including Master of the Tower Armory, Master of the Horse, and finally Earl Marshal.[8]

Even after he reached the pinnacle of his political power as Duke of Northumberland during the reign of Edward, John Dudley still devoted considerable attention to chivalric performance. As Lord President of the Council, he diverted his royal ward and the people of London with numerous tournaments and festivities at court.[9] Northumberland placed his sons prominently in most of these spectacles, providing them with a chance to display their knightly prowess and further enhance the family's prestige.[10]

When Edward died, the Duke's grip on the kingdom was gravely imperiled. He tried to retain it by placing his daughter-in-law, the Lady Jane Grey, on the throne, but this desperate conspiracy collapsed as the country rallied to Mary. The Duke and his sons were imprisoned, attainted, and condemned to death. Northumberland, the Lady Jane, and her husband, Guildford Dudley, were all duly executed. Another son, John, fell ill in the Tower and was released a few days before his death in the fall of 1554. The three surviving sons were luckier. The Duchess of Northumberland was determined to save them, and she worked ceaselessly to ingratiate herself with various Spaniards at the court of Philip and Mary. So did Sir Henry Sidney, who named his newborn son after the King and invited the latter to be the godfather. The Duchess succeeded in winning the release of her sons sometime that fall or winter, and they were pardoned on January 23, 1555, the day after she died.

Once again a tournament marked the reversal of the Dudley family's fortunes and their restoration to favor at court. The brothers' names appear on a score sheet with those of King Philip and his Spanish lords drawn up for a tournament held sometime shortly after their release.[11] The Dudleys owe this surprising reversal to King Philip's efforts to win the loyalty and affection of his English subjects. Animosities between the many Spaniards who accompanied him and the English courtiers were high since each group resented sharing the privileges of attendance on the King. The English felt displaced by these foreign interlopers, and the Spanish in turn were badly abused by their hosts. Within a few months of Philip's arrival, relationships had deteriorated alarmingly: one Spanish gentleman wrote a friend in Salamanca to complain that "the English hate us Spanish, which comes out in violent quarrels between them and us, and not a day passes without some knife-work in the palace between the two nations. There have already been some deaths and last week three Englishmen and a Spaniard were hanged on account of a broil."[12]

In order to provide a more civilized outlet for these hostilities, the Spanish arranged for a tournament to be held at court, issuing their challenge on November 25. Pleased with the success of that event, the King sponsored three more tournaments that winter, admitting the Dudley brothers to the lists after pardoning them. He seems to have been pursuing a conciliatory policy similar to that of Catherine de Médicis, trying as she did to reconcile the hostile factions of his court by turning "real conflict into chivalrous pastime" through these entertainments.[13] Up to a point, antagonisms at court could thus be contained within "the chivalrous design of knightly trial." Robert Dudley and his brothers seized the chance to return to public favor. Just as their father had before them, the younger Dudleys combined chivalric performance with military service, joining Philip's campaign against the French in

1557. Their service was rewarded by the lifting of their attainder, but one brother, Henry, lost his life at the siege of Saint Quentin. After this campaign Robert returned to England, where he lived fairly quietly for the duration of Mary's regime.

Such modest good fortune was a mere prelude to Robert Dudley's meteoric rise during the next regime. When Mary Tudor died in 1558, Dudley greeted Elizabeth's accession with great enthusiasm. Elizabeth made him Master of the Horse, a post once held by his father and older brother; during her coronation progress, Dudley and his brother escorted her through the city, taking the positions closest to her litter (Figure 4).[14] Once again chivalric display was a crucial means to prominence and power. The Master of the Horse was also, as John Neale says, "an honourable and valuable post" that insured proximity to the Queen.[15] During these early years, his attendance upon the Queen was almost constant, and their intimacy scandalized many around them. Dudley's aggressive courtship of Elizabeth following the death of his wife in 1560 did little to diminish the concern of his enemies, who resented the rapid ascent and presumptuous ambitions of this remarkably fortunate favorite.

Dudley's success in chivalric display depended in part on his considerable influence within the College of Arms. His role in that institution shows how the signs system of the ruling class was constantly disputed in a contest with serious political implications. The heralds, who were the principal officials of the college, played a critical role in developing the rites and images of Elizabethan knighthood. They officiated at tournaments, keeping score and awarding prizes; they maintained records of state occasions and magnificent ceremonies; and they traced the ancestry of the nobility and aspiring gentry, assessing claims to ancient distinction and devising genealogies to prove them. The head of the College of Arms was the Earl Marshal—at this point Thomas Howard, the fourth Duke of Norfolk and scion of one of England's most venerable families. He was also "the chief of Lord Robert's enemies," a group that according to the Spanish ambassador included "all the principal people in the kingdom."[16] Some of this hostility derived from

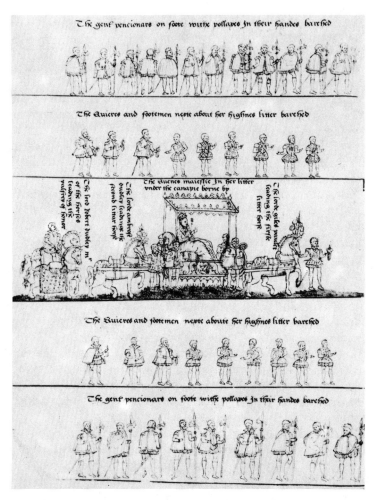

4. Coronation Progress (College of Arms, MS M6, reproduced by permission of the College of Arms).

the contempt of the older nobility for a parvenu. The Earl of Sussex "contemned him as a new upstart, who...could produce no more but two ancestors, namely his father and his grandfather, and those both of them enemies and Traitours to their Country."[17] Some of it was provoked by Dudley's courtship of the Queen. Norfolk threatened "that if Lord Robert did not abandon his present pretensions and presumption he would not die in his bed."[18]

As Earl Marshal, the Duke of Norfolk was determined to throttle the upward mobility of all such upstarts. The College of Arms and its High Court of Chivalry constituted a "powerful tribunal" in which he could exercise "close control on progress from one rung of the social ladder to another."[19] He had secured a new royal charter during Mary's reign and initiated an ambitious set of conservative reforms. A permanent home for heraldic records was established, efforts were made to restrict access to them, and regular visitations were instituted to review the legitimacy of armorial bearings.[20] In 1568 Norfolk tried to consolidate his control still further by drawing up a set of orders prohibiting new grants of arms without a joint decision by the three Kings of Arms—Garter, Clarenceux, and Norroy—as well as the warrant of the Earl Marshal.[21] Norfolk's proposed reforms of the College of Arms were an attempt by the leader of the "ancient aristocracy" to restrict and purify its ranks and gain control of the distribution of honors.

The Duke may have entertained even grander ambitions as Earl Marshal, as David Starkey's recent discovery of an important volume from his library indicates. Starkey found a sixteenth-century manuscript of the *Modus Tenendi Parliamentum* bound together with *Treatises on the Earl Marshal of England*, which belonged to either the third or fourth Duke of Norfolk.[22] In addition to outlining the Marshal's lofty ceremonial duties, the *Treatises* describe his military responsibilities as joint commander, with the Constable, of the Royal Army. The *Modus Tenendi Parliamentum* was also in part a ceremonial treatise, frequently combined with orders of precedence at coronations, funerals, and garter ceremonies as well as the opening of parliaments to form the "corpus of the developing law of chivalry."[23] However, the *Modus* also had significant political implications since it assigned the Marshal and the other high feudal officers great constitutional authority. The treatise contends that the Steward, the Constable, and the Earl Marshal have the power to invoke a parliamentary commission "if there is discord between the King and some magnates, or perhaps between the magnates themselves, whereby the King's peace is undermined, and the people as well as the land is afflicted."[24] Some scholars have seen this claim as a justification in principle of the Barons' Revolt against Edward II, an uprising led by the Steward and Constable.[25] In that crisis those noble magnates may have claimed parliamentary powers even greater than the monarch's. In the seventeenth century the *Modus* became a "controversial" text, used by men like Edward Coke to argue that "there were Parliaments before the Conquest" and thus strengthen "the case for an ancient constitution against the king."[26] In fact, Coke's subsequent acquisition of the volume previously owned by the Duke of Norfolk makes it, as David Starkey suggests, a kind of missing link between medieval constitutional theories and seventeenth-century parliamentary opposition to Stuart autocracy. The passage of this volume from Earl Marshal to parliamentarian shows the continuity of this oppositional tradition throughout the sixteenth century.[27]

These same ideas were revived, as we shall see, in the research commissioned by the Earl of Essex when he became Earl Marshal in 1597. Both Essex and Norfolk rebelled against the crown, and their exalted conception of their own authority, as well as their dismay at its neglect, helped incite them. In 1569 Norfolk was almost drawn into the Northern Rebellion, in which the rebels asserted, among other grievances, that "they were driven of necessity to take Armes, lest the ancient Nobility of England should be trodden vnder foot by new upstarts, and their Countrey deliuered for a prey to strangers."[28] He escaped the disastrous consequences of that upheaval but was then entangled in the conspiracies of Mary Stuart. Norfolk's plan to marry her was initially supported by Leicester, who subsequently disclosed all to the Queen. Norfolk was then charged with treason and executed in 1572. Leicester may have aspired to replace the Duke of Norfolk as Earl Marshal. Leicester's father had held the office under Edward, and Leicester also possessed manuscript copies of the same volume combining the *Modus Tenendi Parliamentum* and the *Treatises on the Earl Marshal of England*.[29] He was instead made deputy to George Talbot, the Earl of Shrewsbury, who was too preoccupied with the task of guarding Mary Stuart to be an effective administrator. After Shrewsbury's death in 1590, "the Marshalcy was put into Commission, with Burghley as principal Commissioner."[30] Elizabeth and her advisers may have decided, after Norfolk's execution for treason, to withhold such a potentially powerful office from her more ambitious nobility.

The Duke of Norfolk's grand ambitions as Earl Marshal were defeated long before his execution. Many of his difficulties were attributable to the contradictions of Elizabethan society, which was both hierarchical and intensely mobile. As a result, the College of Arms was afflicted throughout Elizabeth's reign by a "general uncertainty as to what the heralds' real duty was. How far were they to spurn and how far to facilitate the aspirations of new men to gentility?"[31] The aspirations of new men were largely realized: Lawrence Stone remarks that the "central fact about English social history between 1540 and 1640...was the growth in numbers and wealth of the landed classes and the professions. The number of peers rose from 60 to 160; baronets and knights from 500 to 1400; esquires from perhaps 800 to 3,000; and armigerous gentry from perhaps 5,000 to 15,000."[32] Norfolk's efforts to stem the tide of upward mobility were doomed in the face of such pressures.

At a lower level the Duke's efforts to reform the College of Arms were even further undermined by Leicester's machinations. The latter secured a place within the College for a protégé named Robert Cooke as soon as he could. Cooke was a master of arts from Cambridge who entered Dudley's service near the beginning of Elizabeth's reign. With his patron's help Cooke was appointed to the College of Arms in 1562 without any previous experience or qualifications. Henry Machyn writes that Cooke was first made Blanch Rose Pursuivant on January 25, "the whych he neuer servyd in no plase a-for," only to be elevated to Chester Herald two weeks later.[33] Cooke continued rising through the ranks to become Claren-ceux King of Arms in 1567 and acting Garter King, or chief herald, from 1584 to 1586.[34] Cooke's position was not an easy one because he had to serve two masters. He described the difficulties of trying to please both Dudley and his actual superior, the Earl Marshal, lamenting at one point that "I am frowned out of my friends in the Earl of Leicester's chambers and also of the Earl of Leicester because I resort so much unto the Duke." He also had to endure the contempt of his col-leagues for his servile laxity. William Segar accused him of giv-ing "arms and crests without number to base and unworthy persons for his private gaine," and William Dethick blamed his "violent and subtill...intrusion...into the Office of Garter" on Leicester's interference.[35] Despite these difficulties, Cooke knew where his best advantage lay and remained Leicester's man, producing several spectacular pedigrees for his patron. One, at the College of Arms, traces Elizabeth and Dudley back to the same ancestor, presumably for the purpose of proving them a suitable match.[36] A sumptuously illustrated "Booke of petegrees" at Longleat traces Dudley's descent through more than fifty-seven vellum pages back to the legendary Guy, Earl of Warwick; the latter stands triumphantly above the body of "Colbarne the Danish Giant," holding the trunk and roots of the family tree firmly in his hand (Figure 5).[37]

Cooke was probably the herald responsible for creating an-other heroic image of Leicester in a small but influential antho-logy in the College of Arms. A collection of pictures and texts from late medieval and sixteenth-century tournaments, it accords the Dudley family a prominent role in the revival of chivalry in Tudor times. The anthology contains the earliest extant record of John Tiptoft's fourteenth-century ordinances for "justes of peace royall," and these are illustrated with stylized scenes from an actual tournament, whose events have been altered to "shew the maner of the breaking of the speres" (Figure 6).[38] The picture shows some of the different types of

In the yere of oure Lord 924 this Guy Erle of warwike slew Col=
barne the Danish Giant in hid stead nere winchester After yis
victory y Danes being banishd England the kinge brought y Realme
into one monarchie. This noble Erle of warwike was buried at
a place nere warwike called Guy his Cliff where untill this daye
there remaineth a very auncient monument of him. He had
issue as hereafter appearith in this geanolagie. &

Remeburne
Erle of warwic
son of Guy

Wegeatus
Erle of warwic
son of Reneburne

Ysia Erle
of warwic
son of Wegeatus

Wulgeatus
Erle of warwic
son of Ysia

5. Guy of Warwick and Colbarne the Dane from Robert Cooke's
Genealogy of Robert Dudley, Earl of Leicester (Longleat MS. 249b,
reproduced by permission of the Marquess of Bath, Longleat House,
Warminster, Wiltshire, Great Britain).

6. Combat with lances (College of Arms, MS M6, reproduced by permission of the College of Arms).

blows and attaints described in Tiptoft's rules: thus, we see the first two on the left scoring attaints to the helm, the second pair striking "coronall to coronall," the fifth knight scoring an attaint to the body, and the seventh bearing his opponent down while the eighth shatters his lance. Robert Dudley is identifiable by the ragged staff on his horse bard and the small crescent within it, the younger brother's mark of difference. He is shown scoring the most difficult and exceptional hit— "coronall to coronall." The others can be tentatively identified as William Howard (the lion), Lord Hundson (the swan), Lord Scrope (the "cornish chough,"or blackbird), and Lord Windsor (the unicorn); the eighth is firmly identified as Lord Darcy, whose family includes the bull among their heraldic devices, and the note indicates that he "was not overthrown." The star, or estoile, may be Sussex, whose family device was sometimes a serpent with a star entwined in its tail.[39] All but Sussex ran in a tournament in November 1559 in which Robert Dudley took the challengers' prize and his brother Ambrose won the defenders'. The document commemorates one of the Dudleys' winning performances and uses it to illustrate Tiptoft's ordinances, one of the canonical texts of chivalry.

Two other tournaments in which the Dudleys participated are also included. The Castle of Loyalty (Figure 3) is shown above a proclamation of its challenge presumably because John Dudley was in it. The Spanish challenge of 1554 is included because of its links to the next generation's return to glory. Shorn of its historical context, it becomes a defiant assertion of English patriotism: "Ever in cowrte of great Kynges are wont to com knights of dyvers nations and more to this cowrte of England where is mayntayned knyghthood and feates of armes ioyntly for the service of ladies in more higher degree than in any realme of the worlde."[40] The Spanish are reduced to chivalric pilgrims come "to this cowrte of England" not as its overlords but as knights errant who must be instructed in the demanding requirements of English knighthood. Robert and Ambrose are thus transformed by their happily altered circumstances and the heraldic anthology from marginal survivors into chivalric heroes, their exploits placed amidst a series of exemplary illustrations of contemporary "rites of knighthood."

The illustration of the actual tournament (Figure 6) is itself an emblem of the chivalric compromise and its complexities. It renders the competition artfully symmetrical while suggesting some of the pressures at work beneath its surface. The herald has tactfully rendered each of the Dudleys' contests a draw: since the contestants in each score the same blows as their opponents, each is awarded the same number of points.[41] Yet by doing so, the herald makes the Dudleys the equals of the leading peers of the realm—Robert with a Howard, and Ambrose with a Radcliffe. The impresa shield behind Robert is addressed to the Queen, and it defines their relationship with a subtle mixture of deference and audacity. The picture shows a vine clinging to an obelisk and the motto *te stante virebo*, "you standing I will flourish." It is a symbol of the subject's deference and dependence, as well as a frank proclamation of Dudley's position as a favorite, flourishing only as long as his Queen reigns. Yet it also boldly flaunts the clinging intimacy of his relationship with the Queen to the world. Dudley's "chivalrous designs" managed to combine professions of devotion with a presumption that many of his peers must have found infuriating.

After his wife, Amy Robsart, died in September 1560, Dudley pursued Elizabeth even more aggressively, dramatizing his marital ambitions in a number of chivalric and dramatic pageants. He was an effective patron of the Inner Temple, assisting the templars in a dispute over property, and he was honored as their Christmas Prince at the holiday revels of 1561–62.[42] As the knight Pallaphilos, champion of Queen Pallas and "high Constable marshall of the Knights Templars," Dudley presided over the induction of the knights, a great banquet and tournament, and a series of pageants that may have been enacted or recited, all of which are described in Gerard Legh's *Accedens of Armory*.[43] In the pageants, Perseus rescues Andromeda, Desire woos and marries Dame Beauty, and the event concludes with a masque of "Bewties Dames." The courtship of Beauty by Desire may have been the most evocative because it recalls Henry VIII's siege of Lady Beauty in the Schatew Vert; Ann Boleyn joined Beauty's dames in welcoming the knights of Ardent Desire after they overcame the resistance of Scorn and Disdain.[44]

Legh's treatise and the events it describes show how the symbolic acts and images of Elizabethan chivalry were often exploited for conflicting purposes. Legh dubs himself "Panther Herald" and devises coats of arms and a fictional chivalric order for the aspiring lawyers of the Inner Temple.[45] This was precisely the sort of amateur heraldic activity the Duke of Norfolk sought to suppress because it undermined the control of the College of Arms over the signs system of the social hierarchy. Indeed, the publication of armorial books was frequently condemned for laying open the mysteries of heraldry to the upwardly mobile. When the herald, John Guillim, published a defense of the profession called *A Display of Armory* in 1610, Sir William Segar, the Garter King of Arms at the time, contributed a prefatory poem, but he warned Guillim that "in Arming others, you yourselfe disarme" by providing those outside the College of Arms with the information necessary for devising their own coats of arms.[46] As Frank Whigham has shown, texts of this sort were often "first promulgated by the elite in a gesture of exclusion," but they were "read, rewritten, and reemployed by mobile base readers to serve their own social aggressions." He goes on to point out that tracts on courtesy and honor would have had to be completely suppressed to protect the integrity of elitist values.[47] Norfolk's attempts to impose such controls were once again opposed and eventually defeated by a combination of the upwardly mobile yearnings of the Inner Templars and the ceremonial devices of their patron, Robert Dudley.[48]

Over the next few years Dudley continued to encourage the Queen to marry him in a variety of chivalric entertainments. In March 1565, following a tournament in which he led the challengers, a drama was performed "on the question of marriage, discussed between Juno and Diana, Juno advocating marriage and Diana chastity. Jupiter gave a verdict in favour of matrimony." The Spanish ambassador sat next to Elizabeth throughout the show and reported that at its conclusion "the Queen turned to me and said, 'This is all against me.'"[49] In November of that year the Earl sponsored a tournament at Westminster to celebrate the marriage of his brother Ambrose to Anne Russell, daughter of the Earl of Bedford. After giving the bride in marriage, the Earl of Leicester defended the new couple against a group of knights accompanied by Amazons, fitting opponents to marriage. The opponents aligned themselves with the Queen by fixing their shields on posts below her window and stationing themselves at the tiltyard's "upper Ende next to the Queene."[50] It was not an association she ordinarily welcomed.[51]

At some point during this time Leicester evidently abandoned any serious hope of winning the Queen in marriage, but he could not say so lest "the Queen should...be led to think that he relinquished his suit out of distaste for it...which might cause her, womanlike, to undo him." Leicester never lost sight of his dependence on her favor. The signals of his intentions were therefore deliberately misleading, prompting the Spanish ambassador in 1565 to relay Sir Henry Sidney's assurance that his brother-in-law "had lost hope of his business" and to report a year afterward that Leicester "has not abandoned his pretensions."[52] Indeed, his public courtship of the Queen continued for more than a decade longer until his secret marriage to Lettice Knollys was revealed in 1579.

The grandest show he arranged for the Queen occurred during her summer progress of 1575. "The Princely Pleasures of Kenilworth" combined Arthurian pageantry, courtly compliment, and rustic sport in a motley extravaganza lasting more than two weeks. By this time Leicester's suit had become a courtly formality, but it could still cause tension between them. George Gascoigne's masque of Zabeta included yet another debate between Juno and Diana, and it ended with a speech declaring the necessity "for worthy Queenes to wed"; but it was canceled at the last minute.[53] Indeed, Elizabeth deflated Leicester's pretensions at other points in the "Princely Pleasures." According to "Robert Langham's *Letter*," a comical and clownishly rustic account later suppressed, the Queen was greeted upon her arrival by a Lady of the Lake, who offered Elizabeth "her Lake and poour [power] therein," to which the Queen replied that it was neither the Lord's nor the Lady's to give: "We had thought indeed the Lake had been oours, and doo you call it yoourz noow? Well we wyll heerin common more with yoo hereafter."[54]

Gascoigne's praise of his patron's generosity provoked no such tart rejoinders, incorporating only Echo's benign replies; but though this encounter began well, it ended in a near disaster. Disguised as the Savage Man, Gascoigne asked, "Who gave all these gifts? I pray thee Echo say? / Was it not he who (but of late) this building here did lay?" and Echo obligingly answered, "Dudley." The Savage Man declared it a "worthy gift to be received, and so I trust it shall," and Echo assured him, "It shall."[55] Turning to Elizabeth, he pledged to "submit my selfe / beseeching you to serve," and then, according to Langham's account, Gascoigne "for the more submission brake his tree asunder."[56] When the Savage Man exuberantly completed this gesture by casting away the top of his "tree," one of the pieces nearly hit the Queen's horse. The horse began bucking, and the Queen's footmen subdued him, averting a catastrophe. Langham concludes his description of this mishap with Elizabeth's reassuring words to the alarmed onlookers, "'No hurt no hurt'....Which woords I promis yoo we wear all glad to hear, and took them too be the best part of the play."[57]

This unnerving accident was followed by the cancellation of the masque and the Queen's abrupt departure, events requiring Gascoigne to improvise a new entertainment: the "Queenes Majestie hasting her departure from thence, the Earle commanded master Gascoigne to devise some Farewel worth the presenting, whereupon he himselfe clad like into Sylvanus, God of the Woods." In this new role the poet was obliged to run alongside Elizabeth, recounting the other gods' sorrow at her sudden leave-taking, and lamenting the sufferings of Zabeta's unrequited lovers while she rode to the hunt. When Elizabeth suggested that he "should be driven out of breath by following her horse so fast...Sylvanus humbly besought her Highnesse to goe on...and therewithall protested that hee had rather be her majesties footemen on earth, then a God on horseback in heaven."[58]

George Gascoigne's misadventures at Kenilworth clearly demonstrate, as I have argued elsewhere, the occupational hazards of a poet committed to courtly performance.[59] The accident with the staff, the suppression of his masque, and his breathless and hastily improvised antics as Sylvanus were alternately ludicrous and demeaning. There were certain compensations. Gascoigne was given a royal commission shortly afterward, but it required him to transcribe a text that was not his own. The work was *The Tale of Hemetes the Heremyte*, and it was based on the more modest entertainment presented later that summer by Sir Henry Lee at Woodstock. Perhaps because its heroine rejected marriage for reasons of state, Lee's show was "as well thought of, as any thing ever done before her majestie"——a pointed snub to Leicester's entertainment, which immediately preceded it. The Queen commanded "that the whole in order as it fell, should be brought to her in writing," a task given to Gascoigne.[60] Though Elizabeth may have preferred Lee's more docile and flattering entertainments to Leicester's self-aggrandizing shows, Leicester still persisted in putting her on the spot. In 1578 his nephew, Sir Philip Sidney, composed *The Lady of May* for her majesty's entertainment at Wanstead, another estate of Leicester's. The Queen was again confronted with a marriage choice, but this time she was asked to make the judgment herself. She rejected the suitor favored by Sidney, and hers was, as always, the last word and "best part of the Play." In courtly performance Gascoigne, Sidney, and others repeatedly found their own poetic authority and eloquence nullified by a higher power.

Despite these persistent pressures from Leicester, his relationship with the Queen kept its basic equilibrium largely because she found his sustained courtship more flattering than presumptuous. There were occasionally moments of strain when she felt he went too far. According to Robert Naunton, Elizabeth told Leicester at one point, "I have wished you well, but my favor is not locked up for you that others shall not partake thereof, for I have many servants unto whom I have and will at my pleasure bequeath my favors and likewise reassume the same, and if you think to rule here, I will take a course to see you forthcoming. I will have here but one mistress and no master."[61] Her words are less a rebuke than a reminder of the terms of their relationship and of her relationship to all her powerful subjects; as David Loades says, "the queen distributed her limited bounty, if not fairly, at least with some regard to equity and the legitimate expectations of different parties."[62] William Cecil shrewdly described Leicester's position in 1566 when he wrote, "I think the Queen's majesty's favour to my Lord of Leicester be not so manifest as it was to move men to think she will marry with him and yet his lordship hath favour sufficient."[63]

Leicester finally settled for "favour sufficient," accepting parity rather than preeminence over his peers. The chivalric compromise worked especially well for him as a result. He was also particularly pleased by the outward signs and shows of honor, and these the Queen bestowed on him in abundance. He was given the Order of the Garter early in her reign. In 1564 he was created Baron Denbigh and Earl of Leicester; in 1565 the Queen granted him permission to keep one hundred liveried retainers; the next year both Leicester and the Duke of Norfolk were awarded the French Order of Saint Michel. Norfolk accepted it grudgingly because the French had offered it to Dudley first, and he was sure he was chosen "only to prevent jealousy of Lord Robert's being the only person to receive the order and not from any desire to favour him (the Duke) but on the contrary."[64] Dudley exulted in such honors. In 1571 his protégé, Robert Cooke, now Clarenceux King of Arms, organized his formal investiture into the Order of Saint Michel in Warwick, conducting a progress through the streets of the town. A cloth of estate joining his own arms with the Garter and Saint Michel's golden wreath was set up in Saint Mary's church. Afterward a banquet was held "where very solemnly he keapt the Feast with liberall bountie and great cheare" entirely by himself: in solitary splendor and "without any company," the Earl "kept the state, and was served with many Dishes all covered, and the knees with assaye."[65] For Leicester, it must have been the apex of chivalric ritual.

The belated realization of Leicester's military ambitions subsequently put the chivalric compromise to its severest test. For more than a decade the Earl and his faction had been agitating for intervention in the Netherlands. Leicester finally achieved his desires when he was appointed supreme commander of an expeditionary force in 1585. His qualifications and experience were severely limited. He had not done battle since Saint Quentin thirty years before. Nevertheless, his wealth and prominence made him the logical choice for the job. As Charles Wilson explains, "No one but Leicester could command the combination of private fortune and social prestige which the Queen thought necessary in the man who was to combine the political and military leadership in the Low Countries."[66] Moreover, Leicester could not resist the opportunity to enact the role of chivalric hero in earnest. Unfortunately, the Netherlands expedition only exposed his inadequacies in that role.

In preparing for the expedition, Leicester characteristically concentrated on creating a magnificent impression. Wallace MacCaffrey says that "he assembled around him an entourage which was more like the household of a medieval baron than the headquarters of a Renaissance Captain. For his immediate attendance he had a staff of about 75 persons, including a steward, secretary treasurer, gentleman of the house, comptroller, two gentlemen ushers, four gentlemen of the chamber, two divines, a physician, apothecary and chirugeon."[67] A company of players, trumpeters, and musicians came along to swell the progress further.[68] The Earl was eager to have his scenes of martial grandeur recorded, so he asked Francis Walsingham and Robert Cooke to secure the services of a pursuivant, and William Segar was eventually dispatched despite his "xx excuses."[69]

The impression Leicester created was initially quite favorable, as Dutch hopes ran high. The governor of Willemstad wrote Walsingham shortly before the expedition's departure, applauding the Queen's apparently firm resolve: "I doubt not but that God will bless all heroic enterprises, since he in a way brings back to life the late Prince of Orange in the person of the Earl of Leicester, on whose coming men have fixed their hopes that the affairs of both state and war will be restored to their ancient splendour."[70] After he arrived, the tributes became still more hyperbolic: "The further the earle went up into Holland," writes Holinshed, "the braver the countrie was, and the better his lordship was beloved, as appeared by his more excellent entertainment."[71] Leicester was compared to Moses, called "a second Arthur," and hailed as "a prince above all living" at various points in his progress.[72] These heady tributes finally moved him to accept the office of supreme governor and general, and the title was formally conferred in a solemn investiture ceremony at the Hague where Leicester took an oath "in a chair under a cloth of Estate."[73]

For a brief period it must have seemed the pinnacle of his career, but his triumph was destroyed by the Queen's rage at his presumption. Reports that Lettice Knollys planned to join her newly exalted husband "with such a trayne of ladies and gentylwomen, and such ryche coches, lytters, and syde-saddles, as hir majestie had none suche" further fanned the flames.[74] Elizabeth's rebuke defined their conflict with harsh precision. She insisted on his dependence on her and her alone, calling him "a man raysed uppe by ourselfe, and extra-ordinarily favored by us aboue anie other subject of this land." So great was her anger at this "creature of our owne" that she initially insisted on a formal ceremonial abasement: "He shall make an open and publyke resignation in the place where he accepted the same absolute government, as a thinge done without our privitie and consent;...the election must be revoked with some such solemnytie as the same was pub-lished."[75] Leicester saw his position clearly, and he abjectly yielded, cravenly blaming his subordinates for encouraging him to accept the title.[76] The Queen subsequently relented and declared her willingness to compromise: "It is always thought ...a hard bargayn when both parties are leasers [losers], and so doth fall out in the case betwene us twoo."[77] She was now ready to settle for some qualification rather than a resignation of Leicester's "absolut title." Their compromise was formally enacted at the Garter ceremony in Utrecht on April 23, Saint George's Day, when Leicester marched to the cathedral with an escort of the city's burghers and fifty halberdiers. At the church service he did reverence to a vacant throne and took a place "by certeine degrees lower," and at the banquet after-ward he arranged for another "most sumptuous cloth and chaire of estate for the queenes maiestie, with his armes and stile thereon, and before it a table covered with all things so re-quisit as if in person she had been there"; he also placed himself on a humble stool, "for he would have no chaire."[78] For Leices-ter and the Queen, the chivalric compromise still worked, proving the most effective means for reconciling their conflict-ing interests.

Unfortunately, this ceremonial resolution was of little use in coping with the larger political and military conflicts facing Leicester in the Netherlands. He had difficulty understanding, much less managing, the divisions within the States General, finding it "a monstruous gouernment where so many such heads doe rule."[79] He had problems with his own army as well, quarreling with his seasoned soldiers, such as Sir John Norris, and promoting such unreliable mercenaries as William Stanley and Rowland Yorke, who later betrayed the towns they commanded.[80] Most damaging of all was the Queen's equivocal support for the expedition, which she routinely undercut by inadequate funding, erratic diplomacy, and quarrels with her commander.[81] The last of these difficulties prompted the merchants of Amsterdam to refuse to extend the Earl credit. Leicester wrote to Walsingham to complain of this last indignity, reporting that they interrogated him "to learne what degree I was of in England, and what abilitye, what favour with her majestie, why I would leave Ingland if I had bine a man of so great qualitye as was here reported, ... whether I had anie lands in England, or office but master of the horse, with manie such like questions"; these skeptical businessmen concluded that "in the end ... the quenes majestie would doe nothinge in respect of me; and that thei should find all but a shew of mine owne."[82]

Leicester returned to England in November 1586, and later that winter he joined the enormous funeral cortege honoring his nephew, Sir Philip Sidney. On February 16 seven hundred mourners marched through London to Saint Paul's, an event commemorated in Thomas Lant's beautiful engraving. Sir Francis Walsingham bore the costs of the funeral and paid off his son-in-law's debts, reducing himself to ruin, but the event was organized and "marshalled" by Robert Cooke, Clarenceux King of Arms and Leicester's loyal functionary. F. J. Levy has called the funeral "a grand show of national unity and purpose," but to some extent it was more a show of the *militia*, honoring their own heroic exploits while paying tribute to a fallen peer.[83] The mounted escort included the Earls of Leicester, Huntington, and Essex and Lords Willoughby and North; the last three were veterans of the charge at Zutphen. For Leicester, his nephew's funeral was in part a melancholy substitute for the triumphal return that never occurred.

After returning to the Netherlands in the spring, Leicester

came back to England for good in December 1587 under a cloud of mutual acrimony. In sharp contrast to the splendid pageants that greeted his arrival, there were no ceremonial farewells. Instead, there were hostile medals, including one that showed a hapless Dutchman leaping from the Spaniard's smoke into Leicester's fire.[84] Even greater disgrace threatened at home, where an investigation of the expedition's mismanagement and financial waste was proposed by his enemies, but Leicester spared himself that ordeal by prostrating himself before the Queen.[85] The most damaging consequence of all was the blow to his reputation. For most of his contemporaries, the Netherlands campaign proved, in the words of one, that "Leicester was no great soldier, his nature being more inclinable to ease and delights of the court than to service in the field: though now and then for ambition or hope of gain he would undertake great attempts, as may appear by his wars in the Low Countries, where he spent a great part of the time of his abode in shows of triumph and feasting."[86] Actual warfare exposed the emptiness of Leicester's "rites of knighthood," confirming suspicions that arose even in his own mind that all his magnificence might be "but a shew of mine owne."

For Leicester, such doubts were temporarily dispelled in the last months of his life by the flurry of preparations for the Armada invasion. Shortly after his return from the Netherlands, the Queen assigned him a prominent role in England's land defense, but she still treated him with her customary inconsistency. According to Camden, she was prepared to give him "the highest authority of Lieutenancy under the Queen in the governement of England and Ireland. Which indeede hee had allready obtained, the letters Patents being drawne, had not Burghley and Hatton prevented it, and the Queene in time foreseen the danger of too great a power in one man."[87] Instead, he was appointed "Lieutenant and Captaine generall of ... all our armyes, as shall be levied in any counties of the South partes of this our Realme."[88] Yet even then, as Miller Christy points out, "in spite of the ample powers suggested by his imposing title, he seems to have been given no authority over any of the Queen's forces except those actually in the camp itself."[89] Leicester chafed at these hedged and ambiguous conditions, complaining about his lack of "authority to command any troops if the enemy should land in Kent or Suffolk" and asking that the Lord Chamberlain's commission for commanding the Queen's own military guard "be so worded as not to interfere with his own authority."[90]

Nevertheless, Leicester was ultimately more absorbed in the ceremonial rites of knighthood than its military rights. He knew when to settle for "favour sufficient," and he made the most of his final appointment as an opportunity for triumphant chivalric display. At Tilbury he achieved what Derek Wilson calls "his last and greatest piece of stage-management, the apotheosis of all the court tournaments he had organised over the years."[91] On August 8 he arranged a drill and review of the troops for the Queen at Tilbury, which became the setting for one of her most stirring speeches. After watching their mock combat, Elizabeth assured her soldiers that she would "take up arms myself and be your general, judge, and rewarder of every one of your virtues in the field. I know already for your forwardness you have deserved rewards and crowns; and we do assure you, in the word of a prince, they shall be duly paid you."[92] It was a legendary moment in Elizabethan history, whose parades and spectacles were commemorated in verse by James Aske:

> The Courtiers talke is of the warlike show
> They sawe that day within the royall Campe.
> Some praise the place whereas they camped are:
> Some praise the discipline is us'd therein:
> And othersome the passing forwardnesse
> Of Noble men, and Gentels lying there:
> But all of them do say, the Souldiers are
> Most comely men appoynted well thereto.[93]

Tilbury was the triumph of Elizabethan chivalry as political theater, a brilliant orchestration of martial "forwardness" in a grand show of patriotic fervor and devotion to the Queen; but the country was fortunate that its "warlike show" was not put to the test of an actual invasion.

Tilbury was also Leicester's grand finale, for he died on September 4. He had written a will shortly before in which he considered, at various points, the nature and durability of his accomplishments. The death of his only legitimate son in 1584 meant that his brother Ambrose was his only hope for the endurance of the line. Leicester bequeathed to him a most cherished chivalric honor, yet his pride is qualified by a sense of the honor's transience: "to my deare & noble brother I leave unto him first as deare an affeccon as any brother barre to other...and a George wch hath the french order & the English in one with a playne goulde chayne at it. This token he must keepe in remembrance his brother was of both the orders. And not onlie so but almost the oldest of both the orders in bothe the realmes. But what is yt but vanitie & too much vanitie nowe for me to remember them."[94] Leicester's voice swells with complacency about the venerable dignity of the orders and then cracks with an awareness of the emptiness of all earthly honors. The same mixture of pride and pathos informs his request to be buried "wth as litle pompe or vaine expense of the world as may be" as long as he is interred at Warwick, where "sondrie of my ancestors doe lye."[95] Leicester's ancestral feelings were honored, for his tomb was placed next to Richard Beauchamp's noble monument at Saint Mary's in Warwick.

His memory was little honored otherwise. He was repeatedly defamed in verse and prose that circulated long after his death. Sir Walter Ralegh was supposedly the author of one barbed epigram:

> Here lyes the noble Warryor that never blunted sword:
> Here lyes the noble courtier that never kept his word;
> Here lies his Excellency that governed all the State;
> Here lyes the L. of Leicester that all the world did hate.[96]

Works such as *Leicester's Ghost* revived the slanders of *Leicester's Commonwealth*, the immensely successful attack written during Leicester's lifetime.[97] The ribald "News from Heaven and Hell" reduces the Earl's chivalric exploits to sexual torments, showing Leicester locked in hellish intercourse with a fiery female fiend; despite the pain, "he could not forbeare; especialy haveing bene all his lief a valient cavilere in armes, to geve a charge with his lance of lust against the [ce]nter of her target of proffe." The writer tells us that "his Robinships entertainment" is perpetually celebrated "upon great feastivall dayes" in the underworld.⁹⁸ Thus are Leicester's "rites of knighthood" commemorated in this obscene travesty.

Edmund Spenser's peculiar tribute to his former patron is in some ways more oddly insulting than even these slanders. In *The Ruins of Time*, written in 1591, Spenser dutifully mourns for Leicester and rebukes those whose "Spite bites the dead, that living never baid" (*RT*, line 215). Yet Spenser can provide no positive consolation in the face of these attacks:

> He now is dead, and all his glorie gone,
> And all his greatnes vapoured to nought,
> That as a glasse vpon the water shone,
> Which vanisht quite, so soone as it was sought.
> His name is worne alreadie out of thought,
> Ne anie Poet seekes him to reuiue;
> Yet manie Poets honourd him alive.
>
> (218–224)

From one point of view, Spenser's mournful sense of the transience of Leicester's achievements is entirely conventional. The Earl's honors fail him "Sith all that in this world is great or gaie, / Doth as a vapour vanish, and decaie" (55–56). All worldly glories are vain from the perspective of eternity. Nevertheless, the glories of the dead Sir Philip Sidney are revived, and his "Immortall spirite" lives, in the poem's "Envoy" (673). Even Ambrose Dudley is more fondly recalled as one who "whilst he liued, was of none enuyde, / And dead is now, as liuing, counted deare" (241–242). Spenser clearly discriminates between the achievements of each man, finding that not all is vanity. From another point of view, Leicester was undone by his pursuit of illusions of greatness and glory, empty flatteries of "the courting masker" as evanescent as a vapor. Leicester's aspirations were enormous to begin with, but he kept gradually scaling them down. Aiming at first to be the royal consort, he abandoned that goal to become the leader of the radical Protestant faction and the militant war party. As Wallace MacCaffrey says, "No other Elizabethan politician made such a conspicuously public display of his ambitions nor aimed at such extensive goals." When these ambitions created conflicts and difficulties, Leicester prudently backed away, relinquishing the goals and exulting in the display. Leicester was, as MacCaffrey says, a favorite first and last, his other ambitions never leading all that far.[99] He settled throughout his career for "favour sufficient," and, dazzled by its rewards, he failed to see their lack of substance. For him, the symbolic actions of Elizabethan chivalry eventually became largely symbolic, with few enduring consequences. For a brief time in the Netherlands Leicester worried about other men's regard for his reputation, fearing that "in the end...thei should find all but a show of mine own." From Spenser's viewpoint in *The Ruins of Time*, written after the Earl's death, Leicester's worst fears were realized.

3

Sir Philip Sidney: "The Shepherd Knight"

Sir Philip Sidney was the son of Robert Dudley's sister, and the Earl of Leicester was a powerful influence on his nephew's brief career. Philip's father, Sir Henry Sidney, saw the Dudley connection as the family's greatest distinction, urging him, "Remember, my son, the noble blood you are descended of by your mother's side."[1] When drawing up their own pedigree, the Sidneys employed their distinguished relative's herald, Robert Cooke, who obliged them with characteristic creativity. Cooke began by preparing a bogus genealogical roll tracing the descent of a fictive William de Sydney down to the fourteenth century, which he in turn used as "evidence" for the genealogy he presented as his own—the initial forgery "written on a narrow strip of parchment, which is in a very brittle state. The discoloured appearance of the parchment and the character of the handwriting suggest an attempt to feign antiquity for the Roll; which must have in fact been written little before 1580."[2] Cooke's forgery apparently worked, flattering as it was to the Sidneys' ancestral pride.

Philip's own ancestral pride was particularly fierce, and he was aroused to almost fanatical anger by the slanders leveled against his uncle in *Leicester's Commonwealth*, a book combining reportage on factional maneuvers at court with expert character assassination of the Earl of Leicester. *Leicester's Commonwealth* was published anonymously in Paris in 1584, and Elizabeth's government tried to suppress the book in England, but its circulation in manuscript did grave and lasting damage to Robert Dudley, darkening his reputation even to the present day.[3] He was accused of murder, treason, adultery, and atheism, among other heinous crimes, but the attack most galling to Sidney was aimed at Dudley's lack of long-standing nobility. According to *Leicester's Commonwealth*, Dudley's father was a "buck of the first head," or the first noble of his line, and Leicester himself had aroused the hatred of the "ancient nobility" by his efforts to supplant them.[4] Stung by this slur on "my dead ancestors,"[5] Sidney wrote a *Defence of the Earl of Leicester*, a tract he apparently planned to publish. Taking his father's admonition to heart, Sidney declares, "I am a Dudley in blood, that Duke's daughter's son, and do acknowledge, though in all truth I may justly affirm that I am by my father's side of ancient and always well esteemed and well matched gentry, yet I do acknowledge, I say, that my chiefest honour is to be a Dudley, and truly am glad to have cause to set forth the nobility of that blood whereof I am descended, which, but upon so just cause, without vain glory could not have been uttered: since no man but this fellow of invincible shamelessness would ever have called so palpable a matter in question."[6] Relying in part on the pedigree Robert Cooke prepared for Leicester in 1583, Sidney traces the Dudleys' descent from such venerable families as the Beauchamps, the Talbots, and the Grays.[7] The *Defence of the Earl of Leicester* concludes with a dramatic but futile chivalric gesture. The impassioned defender of family honor challenges his anonymous adversary to a duel within three months' time: "But to thee I say: thou therein liest in thy throat, which I will be ready to justify upon thee in any place of Europe, where thou wilt assign me a free place of coming, as within three months after the publishing hereof I may understand thy mind."[8] Sidney's vehemence abated, and cooler heads evidently prevailed; the *Defence of the Earl of Leicester* was never published, the challenge never promulgated, and the identity of the author of *Leicester's Commonwealth* never revealed.[9]

Some of Sidney's earliest writings were also linked to the Earl of Leicester, and these too met with a dubious reception. The *Lady of May* was a masque devised to entertain the Queen during a visit to Leicester's estate at Wanstead in 1578. The masque concerned that perennial subject of Leicester's entertainments, the marriage question, but here the topic may have figured Leicester's martial rather than marital ambitions. In this case, the Queen was asked to choose between two suitors for the May Lady's hand—a virile and active forester, and a cautious and passive shepherd. Sidney seems to favor the exuberant forester, Therion, and the final song celebrates the triumph of the forest god, Silvanus, over Pan.[10] In 1578 Leicester and his faction were promoting an activist foreign policy by urging military intervention in the Netherlands.[11] Elizabeth found such a course too risky, and her choice of the prudent shepherd may have been a deliberate rebuff to Leicester and his nephew.

Sidney subsequently tried to address the Queen more directly on the subject of marriage, and he met with no more success. In 1579 it appeared that Elizabeth might finally accept the Duke of Alençon, younger brother to the King of France, as a husband. Good Protestants were horrified and their views of the marriage were publicized in a tract entitled "The Discovery of a Gaping Gulf whereunto England is like to be swallowed by another French marriage, if the Lord forbid not the banns by letting her Majesty see the sin and Punishment thereof." The author, John Stubbs, and his printer had their right hands cut off as punishment. Sidney boldly entered the controversy with a letter addressed "To Queen Elizabeth, Touching her Marriage with Monsieur." He probably also served as his uncle's spokesman on this occasion, but his own aversion to Alençon and his mother, Catherine de Médicis, were rooted in the latter's role in the Saint Bartholomew's Day Massacre, an event Sidney witnessed during his first visit to the Continent. His distrust of this "Frenchman, and a Papist...the son of the Jezebel of our age," was already deeply ingrained.[12] In his letter Sidney declares his "unfeigned love" for the Queen, but he warns her that her subjects' love was always conditional: "Virtue and justice are the only bands of the people's love. And as for that point, many princes have lost their crowns, whose own children were manifest successors."[13] It is an extraordinary threat, one that could hardly endear the author to the Queen. Sidney's politesse and higher status may have spared him the fate of John Stubbs, but almost all advice on marriage was offensive to the Queen.[14]

Shortly after he wrote the letter, Sidney confronted the Queen directly in an extraordinary showdown on the rights of subjects—rights he asserted by resorting to "the rites of knighthood." A quarrel with the Earl of Oxford over the use of a tennis court led to a formal challenge to a duel. The Privy Council intervened to block it, but Sidney insisted on following through, so the Queen herself interceded. Elizabeth sought to put him in his place, according to Sir Fulke Greville. In the latter's admiring account of this event, the Queen tries to remind Sidney of "the difference between earls and gentlemen; the respect inferiors ought to their superiors," but Sidney retorts "that place was never intended for privilege to wrong."[15] Greville declared that Sidney established here "a latitude for subjects to reserve native and legal freedom by paying humble tribute in manner, though not in matter, to them." In his own life, however, he was both more tractable and more successful in his relations with the monarch; indeed, for himself, he finally doubted "whether there be any latitude left—more than humble obedience—in these nice cases between duty and selfness in a sovereign's service."[16] Sidney also had to yield to his sovereign's authority and forgo the duel, and shortly afterward he withdrew to his sister's estate at Wilton.

In 1581 Sidney tried a somewhat different approach to courtly politics, now that he was determined to play more strictly by its rules. His New Year's gift to the Queen was a diamond-studded whip, the perfect token of courtly discourse. Instead of straightforward exhortation, he employs a device as ambiguous as Dudley's impresa shield, subtly suggesting both submission and resentment. He resumed an active public life as a member of Parliament and a frequent performer in court spectacle, participating in three tournaments and two marriage pageants. The grandest of these was *The Four Foster Children of Desire*, an entertainment combining tilting with an allegorical assault on "The Fortress of Perfect Beauty," the gallery housing the Queen. The four challengers, or "foster children," were the Earl of Arundel, Lord Windsor, Sir Fulke Greville, and Sir Philip

Sidney. Sidney was the challengers' standard bearer because his men wore the "poesie, or sentence" justifying their assault, and the dramatic idea behind the tournament was probably his.[17] In organizing this spectacular chivalric fete, Sidney was following his uncle's lead. His magnificent entry is described in an account of the tournament published shortly afterward:

> Then proceeded M. Philip Sidney, in very sumptuous maner, with armor part blewe, & the rest gilt & engraven, with foure spare horses, having caparisons and furniture veri riche & costly, as some of cloth of gold embroidred with pearle, and some embrodred with gold and silver feathers, very richly & cunningly wrought, he had foure pages that rode on his foure spare horses, who had cassock coats & venetian hose al of cloth of silver, layd with gold lace, & hats of the same with golde bands, and white fethers, and eache one a paire of white buskins. Then had he a thirtie gentlemen and yeomen, & foure trumpetters, who were all in cassocke coats and venetian hose of yellow velvet, laid with silver lace, yellowe velvet caps with silver bands and white fethers, and every one a paire of white buskins. And they had uppon their coates, a scrowle or bande of silver, which came scarfewise over the shoulder, and so downe under the arme, with this poesie, or sentence written upon it, both before and behinde, Sic nos non nobis.[18]

Sidney's entry, with its four trumpeters, a page, and a liveried entourage of thirty, seems as extravagantly self-aggrandizing, and the siege as aggressive, as any of his uncle's performances. Nevertheless, their styles are significantly different.

The Four Foster Children of Desire addresses the issue of marriage more subtly and deferentially than Sidney's earlier works. The show begins with a comically innocuous attack on the Queen's gallery by a wooden and canvas "Rowling trench" (*FFC*, p. 68). Musicians concealed within this contraption "cunningly conveyed divers kinde of most excellent musicke against the castle of Beauty" (p. 69). After the "trench or Mounte of earth was mooved as nere the Queenes Majestie as might be" (p. 71), two of Sidney's songs were sung, the first by a boy imploring the Queen to "Yeelde, Yeelde, o Yeelde" and the second by another, representing the defenders, defying their assault.[19] Afterward, "two Canons were shott off, the one with sweet powder, and the other with sweete water, very odoriferous and pleasaunt, and the noyse of the shooting was very excellent consent of mellodie within the Mounte: And after that, was store of prettie scaling ladders, and the footemen threwe Flowers and such fancies against the walles, with all such devices as might seeme fit shot for Desire" (pp. 72–73). The device evokes the symbolically erotic associations of siege warfare as well as earlier Tudor pageants of Beauty and Desire, including Henry VIII's masque of "Ardent Desire," in which Anne Boleyn made her debut, and Dudley's Christmas revels at the beginning of Elizabeth's reign. In both of these earlier shows, however, the siege was successful, and the masque concluded with a dance uniting the lady with the triumphant knight. In *The Four Foster Children of Desire* the challengers' aggression is muted, and their siege fails. The Fortress of Perfect Beauty proves "Impregnable" (p. 82), and they graciously concede defeat.

The position of the foster children is ambiguous from the beginning. They are, first of all, plaintive children rather than domineering suitors, and they desire only to be fostered, or nursed. This figure is one of Sidney's most striking, first appearing in *Certain Sonnet* 6, where Desire is a baby crying for pap, and beauty is a nurse whose care fails to satisfy. The figure is reworked in *Astrophil and Stella* 71, where "Desire still cries give me some food" and fails to obtain it. In both instances Desire is more helpless than aggressive. The foster children are also virtuously submissive, although their adversaries do not understand this. The Queen's defenders compare her to the sun and accuse the foster children of seeking their own gain in their assault on her castle: "Sir Knights, if in besieging the sunne, ye understood what you had undertaken, ye would not destroye a common blessing for a private benefit" (*FFC*, p. 75). The defenders urge them to "desist, sithe it is impossible to resist, content your selves with the sunnes indifferent succor" (p. 75). They do in fact desist, showing themselves capable of the altruism demanded of the true lover in *Astrophil and Stella* 61:

> That who indeed infelt affection beares,
> So captives to his Saint both soule and sence,
> That wholly hers, all selfnesse he forbeares,
> Thence his desires he learnes, his live's course thence.

However, they have announced their virtuous self-denial from the tournament's start. The "poesie, or sentence" worn by Sidney's entourage declares "Sic nos non nobis": "we [do or act] thus not for ourselves" (*FFC*, p. 70).

The righteous pathos of the challengers is one of the central points of the complex allegory of *The Four Foster Children of Desire*. At one level, the challengers' surrender can be seen as a tactful apology for the presumptuous interference in the Queen's marriage choice by Sidney and Leicester. At the same time, the tournament, which was devised for the entertainment of the French ambassadors, slyly denies the Queen to Alençon and every other suitor now that Leicester is out of the running, for Alençon must also content himself "with the sun's indifferent succor."[20] Finally, the allegory delicately hints at the political constraints on the Queen. She has no choice regarding a husband because "when Beawtie yeeldeth once to desire, then can she never vaunt to be desired again" (p. 80). Desire persists only as long as it is unrequited. By the middle of Elizabeth's reign the familiar romantic paradox had acquired an inescapable political significance for her as she rejected the last serious candidate for her hand.

Running through all these compliments is an undertone of resentment felt by those who cry futilely for succor. Patronage is the issue figured by this metaphor of fosterage. Sir Robert Naunton uses the same metaphor to describe the demands of the Earl of Essex, saying he "drew in fast like a child sucking on a uberous breast."[21] Uberous, linked to udder, means rich, full, and abundant, but in practice, Elizabeth seldom proved especially "uberous" to those dependent on her. Sir Francis Bacon remarks instead on "her wonderful art in keeping servants in satisfaction, and yet in appetite"; elsewhere he says that she "allows of amorous admiration but prohibits desire."[22] *The*

Four Foster Children of Desire dramatizes this tantalizing situation, showing how its victims are pathetically "weake in Fortune"; they clamor for their "desired patrimonie" (*FFC*, p. 66) as well as maternal nurture, but what they receive is meager. Perfect Beauty "yeeldes continuall foode to all her foes, and though they feede not fat therewith, yet must they either feede theron or fast" (p. 79). The resentments intimated in *Certain Sonnet* 22, Sidney's only poem explicitly praising the Queen, resurface here: Elizabeth's admirers are in thrall to a lady "On whome all love, in whom no love is plaste."

The Four Foster Children of Desire consciously enacts the chivalric compromise. The participants declare "their most humble hearted submission" (*FFC*, p. 83), but their prowess in the tiltyard still "give[s] such true proofes of their valler, as at least shal make their desires more noble" (p. 68). Moreover, the tournament resolves the conflict between the Queen and her subjects since the latter apologize for interfering in the French marriage suit while righteously denying the Queen to all suitors. Finally, its allegory is a small masterpiece of what Louis Montrose calls "celebration and insinuation," one that simultaneously compliments and criticizes the Queen.[23] The impresa's insistence on the challengers' selflessness and the broader intimations of the Queen's cruel indifference are as slyly ambiguous as the diamond-studded whip. Less overtly hostile than the tournament depicted in Christopher Marlowe's *Edward II*, *The Four Foster Children of Desire* also masks its aggressions behind obsequious speeches. In Marlowe's play the King easily grasps the significance of the contestants' impresas, asking, "Can you in words make showe of amitie, / And in your shields display your rancorous minds?"[24] If the Queen discerned any comparable rancor behind Sidney's "show of amitie," she let it pass on this occasion.

Because it went so smoothly, *The Four Foster Children of Desire* was, in one sense, Sidney's most successful courtly performance. Nevertheless, it still did not produce the desired results, revealing the practical limits of "the rites of knighthood." Sidney returned to court in 1581, hoping to secure profitable employment, but he only met with further disappointments.

The first occurred sometime before June when Lettice Knollys gave birth to a son. Prior to this event Sidney had been Leicester's sole heir, but he now found himself supplanted. Sidney could still dramatize his loss of a "desired patrimony" in the tiltyard by riding in a tournament with the device, "~~SPERAVI~~, thus dashed through to shew his hope therein was dashed."[25] However, by the end of the year his frustrations became harder to accept as he found himself entangled in a "comber of debtes."[26] He had followed his uncle's lead by staging *The Four Foster Children of Desire*, but Leicester's relationship to the Queen was harder to emulate. Sidney's frustration with his mentor is evident in a letter written to Leicester late in 1581: "Well my Lord your Lordeshippe made me a courtier do you think of it as seemes best unto you."[27] By year's end, according to Wallace, Sidney withdrew again from court and "remained at Wilton for Christmas, and the fact that he did not present a New Year's gift to the Queen, and that his name does not appear in the lists of challengers or defenders in the great royal tournament of January 1st which was held in honour of the Duke D'Alençon, makes it probable that he extended his visit into the New Year."[28] Following the activities of the previous year, this seems like a conspicuous absence.

Sidney's attitude toward the court at this point is just as ambiguous as his movements. Fifteen eighty-two is the year he composed *Astrophil and Stella*, and these sonnets are often seen as a turning away from the "busie wits" at court.[29] Arthur Marotti argues that the sequence is directed to a coterie audience that provides "an imaginative and social retreat more hospitable" than the court.[30] Annabel Patterson sees evidence of a growing alienation from court in the *New Arcadia*, whose revisions suggest a "loss of confidence in indirect or covert discourse, or in messages accommodated to the forms of Elizabethan courtship."[31] A. C. Hamilton traces Sidney's disillusionment with the court back to an earlier stage, contending that "by 1579 Sidney was becoming more estranged from the court, imaginatively if not physically," because of his failure to find employment. In Hamilton's view, all Sidney's serious writing from the *Old Arcadia* onward is the work of "a poet writing privately, apart from the court even while he belongs to it. From 1580 until the final year of his life, the pattern is more definite: his essential life took place in his writings, however outwardly busy he may have been in affairs at court."[32]

There is certainly ample evidence of hostility toward the court in all of Sidney's works, but the movement of his mind in both his literature and his life is not one of progressive disillusion but continual oscillation. The pastoral havens of literature beckon, but the court proves inescapable for him. In the first eclogues of the *Old Arcadia*, Musidorus sings:

> that better it is to be private
> In sorrows torments, then, tyed to the pompes of a pallace,
> Nurse inwarde maladyes, which have not scope to be
> breath'd out.

At this point in the work, the hero has assumed his pastoral disguise and prefers to "disburden a passion / ... by the helpe of an outcrye: / Not limited to a whispringe note, the Lament of a Courtier."[33] Sidney may have felt this way as well, but he still chose to take a prominent role in *The Four Foster Children of Desire*, one of the reign's grandest "pompes" shortly afterward, adapting his complaints there to the "whispringe note, the Lament of a Courtier."

Sidney's disaffection resurfaces in "Two Pastorals," written after 1581. The first is a celebration of true friendship with Fulke Greville and Edward Dyer, and the second, a frankly stated "Disprayse of a Courtly Life." The speaker of the "Disprayse" begins by describing his escape from the oppressive heat of the sun into a pleasant, flourishing wood:

> Walking in bright *Phoebus'* blaze
> Where with heate oppreste I was,
> I got to a shady wood,
> Where greene leaves did newly bud.
> And of grasse was plenty dwelling,
> Deckt with pyde flowers sweetely smelling.[34]

Elizabeth had been identified with the sun in *The Four Foster Children of Desire*, and here the speaker is "oppreste" by the blazing heat and light of courtly life. The "shady wood" of pastoral provides partial relief for another courtier, one who turns out to be a thinly disguised version of Sidney:

> In this wood a man I met,
> On lamenting wholly set:
> Rewing change of wonted state,
> Whence he was transformed late,
> Once to Shepheard's God retayning,
> Now in servile Court remayning.

The man laments his "change" from a retainer of the "Shepheard's God," Pan, and his return to the "servile Court." In the treacherous world of the court he cannot share his sufferings with anyone, and he finds solace only in pastoral solitude, venting his griefs to "a senceless tree." The shepherd misses his "old mates" who spent their time "never striving, but in loving," and he complains that he is poorly equipped for the competition and conflict of court life.

Sidney then distinguishes between the true love he feels for his friends and the deceptive "art of Love" required at court, insisting that he also lacks the skill needed for such an art:

> Therefore shepheardes wanting skill,
> Can Love's duties best fulfill:
> Since they know not how to faine,
> Nor with Love to cloake Disdaine,
> Like the wiser sorte, whose learning,
> Hides their inward will of harming.

The most repellent feature of the court was its enforcement of a code in which Love is used "to cloake Disdaine." Yet despite his aversion to such pretense, he is still "in servile court remaining."

Sidney's evident disillusion with "the rites of knighthood" is manifest in a poem recently discovered by Peter Beal and attributed to Sidney. It precedes two other poems linked to the occasion of the Accession Day tilt in the Ottley manuscript, and its references to the event are detailed and depressing:

> Waynd from the hope wch made affection glad
> to show it self in himnes of delight
> yet highly pleased wth thos conceipts I had

made me in deserts grow a desert knighte
that synce no new impression shuld take mee
vnto myne old I might the freer bee
Ocasion deare the nurse or hand of hope
by ecchoes sound made knowne yor enitry daye
Affection fond to take his former scope:
Make me of ioye tread on this comonwaye
Myne armor barke & mosse of faded tree
My speares wild poles my end to love and see.

The verses were "inclosed in a tree sealed with a grene leaf," addressed "to her that is mrs of men, . . . & Sainte of the sabaoth," and accompanied by an impresa of a "tree, the one half springing ye othr half dying & this word hoc ordine fata. Such be ye corse of Heavens."[35] The poem's metaphoric links to *The Four Foster Children of Desire* are especially interesting. In its description of a knight who is weaned from hope, it pursues the themes of nurturing and frustration, hope and despair. In the earlier tilt the "long haples, now hopeful fostered children of Desire" charged into the lists despite the efforts of their "dry nurse Dispaier [who] indevered to waine them from it" (*FFC*, p. 67). In the poem Despair has almost triumphed, depriving the event of the high-spirited ardor that "made affection glad / to show itself" in the annual tournament. The speaker is still "pleasd wth those conceipts I had [that] made me in deserts grow a desert knight." In his desolate, solipsistic contemplation, cut off from "new impression," he resembles Philisides in the *Old Arcadia*, who also sings "in those desert places."[36]

Hope and affection still persist, with affection still "fond to take his former scope"; but the double meaning of "fond" suggests the foolishness of this return to an old rut. Line 10 gives lip service to the knight's "ioye" while subverting this impression with a tone of weary resignation. The same line repeats the verb *make* for the fourth time, reinforcing the sense of pervasive coercion and passivity. The decision to "tread on this comon waye" hardly conveys any pleasure in the quest. This Accession Day tilt presents the image of a crowded treadmill, and the tone of weary, helpless resignation is confirmed by an impresa of a half-dead tree and the motto *hoc ordine fata*.

Hope and affection are only kept alive by the "nurse" Occasion rather than Desire. Occasion is, in one sense, the poem's central topic, the cause and opportunity for public celebration and performance, summoning the speaker from the "deserts" of private reflection. Nevertheless, as the melancholy tone of the poem indicates, such occasions must have seemed increasingly inadequate. Greville writes that Sidney "never was magistrate, nor possessed of any fit stage for eminence to act upon."[37] That the tiltyard at Whitehall provided the only public stage, the only alternative to pastoral withdrawal, for so much of his career must have grated on Sidney at various points. Nevertheless, for all his melancholy posing, he kept coming back to the tiltyard. His impresa shield of 1584 displayed a buoyantly optimistic motto, countering the gloom of "Waynd from the hope" as well as the bitter complaint that his uncle had "made me a courtier." In the 1584 tournament, instead of complaining that his activities or identity were "made" by another, he resolutely declared, *"Inveniam viam aut faciam*—I will make or find a way."[38] Sidney decided in his *Apology for Poetry* that the poet's most "high and incomparable" title was "maker," and he remained determined to make his own way in life as well as literature.[39]

In Sidney's literature it becomes obvious that his melancholy pose was an integral part of his chivalric persona and style. Like the attraction to pastoral withdrawal, this attitude was incorporated into his tiltyard devices and chivalric fiction, complicating and enriching them. Instead of opposing the conventions of Elizabethan chivalry, these postures were part of the chivalric repertoire. In the *Old Arcadia* Sidney's fictional persona, Philisides, is a sorrowful lover and stranger shepherd, whose thoughts are supposedly far from "courtly pomps" (*OA,* p. 335), but in the *"New" Arcadia* he returns as a shepherd knight to join in the annual Iberian tilts devised to celebrate the royal wedding anniversary:

> The time of the maryinge that Queene was every year, by the extreame love of her husband & the serviceable love of the Courtiers, made notable by some publike honours, which indeede (as it were) proclaymed to the worlde, how deare she was to the people. Among other, none was either more grate-

full to the beholders, or more noble in it selfe, than justs, both
with sword and launce, mainteined for a seven-night together:
wherein that Nation dooth so excell, bothe for comelines and
hablenes, that from neighbour-countreis they ordinarily com,
some to strive, some to learne, and some to behold.[40]

Philisides's entry into the lists is a paradoxical display of pastoral magnificence. He is announced

with bagpipes in steed of trumpets; a shepheards boy before
him for a Page, and by him a dosen apparelled like shepherds
for the fashion, though rich in stuffe, who caried his launces,
which though strong to give a launcely blow indeed, yet so
were they couloured with hooks neere the mourn, that they
pretily represented shephooks. His own furniture was drest
over with wooll, so enriched with Jewels artificially placed, that
one would have thought it a mariage between the lowest and
the highest. His *Impresa* was a sheepe marked with pitch, with
this word *Spotted to be knowne*. And because I may tell you out
his conceipt (though that were not done, till the running for
that time was ended) before the Ladies departed from the
windowes, among them there was one (they say) that was the
Star, wherby his course was only directed.

(NA, pp. 284–285)

Philisides jousts against the expert Lelius, "who was knowne
to be second to none in the perfection of that Art" and who
magnanimously lets his youthful adversary win (p. 285).
Frances Yates and others have noted the clear references to
Elizabeth's Accession Day tilts as well as the more specific allusion to an actual combat with Sir Henry Lee.[41]
    Despite his own and his characters' supposed estrangement
from "courtly pomps," Sidney's fiction remains firmly bound
by their supposedly superficial splendors. His description of the
Iberian jousts and similar events incorporates the customs and
practices of contemporary tournaments in loving and expert
detail.[42] At the same time, the corruption of the Iberian court
makes its annual festivities a hypocritical sham. The marriage
the tournaments celebrate has allowed the Queen, Andromana,
to dupe her uxorious, sybaritic husband and seize control of
the kingdom. Having first seduced the King's son, Plangus, the

wicked Andromana then banishes him and replaces him as heir to the throne with her own son, Palladius. When the two heroes of the *New Arcadia*, Pyrocles and Musidorus, arrive in her kingdom, she attempts to seduce them and imprisons them for resisting. They are released during the Iberian jousts where they join her son, Palladius, and help him win the day's prize. When the honorable Palladius tries to help the heroes escape, he is killed by the troops Andromana sends to pursue them, and Andromana, overcome by grief and shame, kills herself. As David Norbrook has remarked, "the imagery of courtly ceremonial is associated with violence and imprisonment rather than delight" in the *New Arcadia*, giving the work what he calls an oddly "claustrophobic atmosphere."[43] Feelings of claustrophobia suffuse the episodes of Book II, as the protagonists' martial prowess and chivalric heroism prove increasingly ineffective. The adventures of Pyrocles and Musidorus culminate in a chaotic sea battle, which is terrifyingly claustral: "For the narrownesse of the place, the darkenesse of the time, and the uncertainty in such a tumult how to know friends from foes, made the rage of swordes rather guide, then be guided by their maisters" (*NA*, p. 305).

Book III initially promises to break free of this narrative impasse. The book focuses primarily on the war between King Basilius and the rebel Amphialus, and their struggle has a serious and unsettling political significance. The "justification" of his rebellion published by Amphialus draws heavily on Huguenot theories of the subaltern magistrate, theories Sidney would have known through his acquaintance with François Hotman's *Franco-Gallia* and with the *Vindiciae Contra Tyrannos*, presumably written by his friend Philippe de Mornay. Both works oppose to the potentially tyrannical powers of the crown the constitutional authority of the nobility, setting forth its right to legitimate resistance.[44] Amphialus also argues that responsibility for the country should be shared by the ruling classes: "The care whereof did kindly apperteine to those, who being subalterne magistrates and officers of the crowne, were to be employed as from the Prince, so for the people" (*NA*, p. 372). This responsibility requires that "the weale publicke was more to be regarded, then any person, or magistrate that thereunto was ordeined" (p. 372). Thus, "the duetie which is owed to the countrie, goes beyond all other dueties" (p. 371), superseding older loyalties to the monarch. Such rational abstraction subverts and demystifies traditional bonds, such as "all tender respects of kinred" and "long-helde opinions," because these are simply oppressive deceits, "rather builded upon a secreate of governement, then any ground of truth" (p. 371).

Having established these general principles, Amphialus applies them to the political crisis in Arcadia. Because Basilius has "given over al care of government" and neglects the "good estate of so many thousands," the country founders in a "dangerous case" (*NA*, p. 372). He proposes to restore order by taking control himself, a move justified by claims of blood as well as political necessity: Amphialus is "descended of the Royall race, and next heire male" (p. 372). The duly appointed regent, Philanax, is denigrated as "a man neither in birth comparable to many, nor for his corrupt, prowde, and partiall dealing, liked of any" (p. 372). The inconsistencies of the theory begin to show at this point, as Amphialus's "justification" tries to have it both ways, alternately denying and asserting traditional standards of legitimacy. Such inconsistencies were inherent in assertions of the rights of subaltern magistrates, whose radical and revolutionary impulses were muted by a desire to preserve their place in the social hierarchy. Yet for all its logical weaknesses, Amphialus's justification of rebellion has a disturbing polemical power rarely matched in Elizabethan literature.

Amphialus's preparations for battle also show a strategic clarity and intelligence uncommon in chivalric romance:

> Then omitted he nothing of defence, as wel simple defence, as that which did defend by offending, fitting instruments of mischiefe to places, whence the mischiefe might be most liberally bestowed. Nether was his smallest care victuals, as wel for the providing that which should suffice both in store & goodnesse, as in well preserving it, and wary distributing it, both in quantitie, and qualitie; spending that first which would keepe lest.
>
> (*NA*, p. 373)

Once the battle begins, Amphialus is carried away by its excitement; but while the protagonist loses his sense of its larger ends, the author does not, at least not immediately. Sidney assigns a more practical perspective to an "olde Governour" of Amphialus and allows him to interrupt the action. The older authority breaks up a fight between his former charge and a Black Knight, wounding the latter warrior and killing his horse: "Amphialus cried to him, that he dishonoured him: You say well (answered the olde Knight) to stande now like a private souldier, setting your credite upon particular fighting, while you may see Basilius with all his hoste, is getting betweene you and your towne" (p. 393). The old governor rebukes him once again when Amphialus accepts another opponent's challenge to single combat, one whose motto is, "The glorie, not the pray" (p. 416). This irresponsible subordination of practical to chivalric ends is condemned by the seasoned veteran who accuses Amphialus of seeking "rather...the glorie of a private fighter, then of a wise Generall" (p. 414). The harsh and ugly violence of the opening scenes of the war seems to confirm Sidney's agreement with the old governor's point of view because he deliberately strips away the glorious facade of chivalry:

> For at the first, though it were terrible, yet Terror was deckt so bravelie with rich furniture, guilte swords, shining armours, pleasant pensils, that the eye with delight had scarce leasure to be afraide: But now all universally defiled with dust, bloud, broken armours, mangled bodies, tooke away the maske, and sette foorth Horror in his own horrible manner.
>
> (p. 392)

Nevertheless, despite these initial glimmers of critical insight, the *New Arcadia* remains bound by the conventions of chivalric romance. The old governor soon disappears from the narrative, and Amphialus can blithely ignore his admonitions. Oblivious to the requirements of supply, fortification, and military command, Amphialus concentrates instead on the decorations of his horse and armor in his efforts to impress his beloved. The war itself shrinks to a series of single combats, most involving Amphialus, and it regains the chivalric glamor lost in the first battle. In Sidney's eyes, combat presents a beautiful spectacle even when its outcome is painfully tragic. Amphialus easily defeats the "knight of the Tombe," only to discover that he has slain the lady, Parthenia. The wife of a knight killed in a previous encounter, she yearns only to join her husband in death, and she dies thanking Amphialus for this "service" (*NA*, p. 447). Amphialus is overwhelmed by feelings of "grief, compassion, & shame," but Sidney's description of the corpse is oddly exquisite:

> her necke, a necke indeed of Alablaster, displaying the wounde, which with most daintie blood laboured to drowne his owne beauties; so as here was a river of purest redde, there an Iland of perfittest white, each giving lustre to the other; with the sweete countenance (God-knowes) full of an unaffected languishing: though these thinges to a grosly conceaving sense might seeme disgraces; yet indeed were they but apparailing beautie in a new fashion, which all looked-upon thorough the spectacles of pittie, did ever encrease the lynes of her naturall fairenes.
>
> (p. 447)

The cruel marks of her injuries might shock or horrify "a grosly conceaving sense," but the discerning esthete sees that they only make the victim more beautiful. Such chivalric equanimity imposes an elegant order on the dreadful mayhem of warfare, allowing its adherents to die a "beautiful" death, but it tends to lose sight of the larger purpose of war in its focus on the individual warrior and his encounters. Amphialus's struggle forfeits its strategic coherence as it degenerates into a string of self-contained, inconsequential contests.

The political aims professed in Amphialus's "justification" are similarly blurred. Despite its inconsistencies, that statement made claims for the nobility's subaltern authority that were truly revolutionary. However, responsibility for these unorthodox ideas is exclusively assigned to Amphialus's wicked mother, Cecropia, who finally dies for her role in kidnapping the princesses. The son's actual motives turn out to be entirely romantic. Like the heroes, Pyrocles and Musidorus, he also loves one of the daughters of King Basilius, but he resorts to open war rather than subterfuge to free them from their father's control. Moreover, his love is unrequited, driving him to ever more desperate measures. Amphialus's hopeless passion wins the sympathy of his harshest enemies, including the regent, Philanax, who says that his "fault passed is excusable, in that Love perswaded, and youth was persuaded" (*NA*, p. 401). His love for Philoclea inflames and then mollifies his aggression, "making all his authoritie to be but a footestoole to Humbleness" (p. 370). Romantic pathos finally supplants rebellious ambition. Enraged and grieved by the discovery of his mother's abuse of their captives, including his beloved Philoclea, Amphialus tries to kill himself and fails, presenting a "pittiful spectacle, where the conquest was the conquerors overthrow" (p. 494).

Caught between conflicting impulses of aggression and self-destruction, Amphialus is a typical Sidney hero. Pyrocles, the main protagonist of the *New Arcadia*, also oscillates between defiance of authority and resignation to the defeat of his desire. Toward the end of the *New Arcadia* he too bungles his attempt at suicide, his resistance to Basilius's authority overwhelmed by romantic pathos, but his last scene is more heroic than Amphialus's. At the end he rises to do battle with one last foe. Sidney's description of their struggle breaks off in mid-sentence, leaving the *New Arcadia* unfinished.

In several senses Sidney resembles his heroes, and the end of his book resembles his own. Sir Philip shared his characters' youthful energy, passionate activism, and high ideals. He was as determined as they were "to imploy those gifts esteemed rare in them to the good of mankind" (*NA*, p. 206), but when he did so, he too found himself entangled in intractable difficulties and conflicts with authority. As a result, many of his undertakings, including his last, resembled his heroes' adventures, which were "not so notable for any great effect they perfourmed, yet worthy to be remembred for the unused examples therein" (p. 206). Finally, both stories, Sidney's and the *New Arcadia*'s, are cut off in the middle with stirring scenes of chivalric heroism, their larger contradictions remaining unresolved.

Sidney's "desyre for the beeing busied in a thing of som serviseable experience" grew increasingly urgent after the disappointments of 1581.[45] He attempted various projects, including joining Drake's voyage to the New World, but, as Fulke Greville says, "Sir Philip found this and many other of his large and sincere resolutions imprisoned within the plights of their fortunes that mixed good and evil together unequally."[46] The Netherlands expedition seemed the answer to his prayers since he could finally take his rightful place as a military commander in the sacred struggle against Spain, confident in the righteousness and ultimate triumph of the Protestant cause: "For me thinkes I see the great work indeed in hand, against the abusers of the world, wherein it is no greater fault to have confidence in mans power, then it is to hastily to despair of Gods work." Sidney's problems with the Queen persisted since she was apt "to interpret everything to my disadvantage," and he was eager to deny her suspicions on a particular point: "I understand I am called very ambitious and prowd at home, but certainly if thei knew my ha[rt] thei woold not altogether so judg me."[47] Throughout his life Sidney was hobbled by an inability to acknowledge his own ambitions.

Once in the Netherlands, Sidney proved to be a responsible and effective general, paying close attention to matters of finance and supply, discipline and tactics. Greville's description of his capture of Axel praises him accordingly:

> For instance, how like a soldier did he behave himself, first, in contriving, then in executing, the surprise of Axel, where he revived that ancient and severe discipline of order and silence in their march, and after their entrance into the town, placed a band of choice soldiers to make a stand in the market-place, for security to the rest that were forced to wander up and down by direction of commanders, and, when the service was done, rewarded that obedience of discipline in every one liberally out of his own purse.[48]

His father's secretary, Edmund Molyneux, asserted that

> his advice for the service intended at Gravelin (dissenting in opinion from others, who were thought the most expert capteins and best renowned and sorted souldiours) gave such a sufficient proofe of his excellent wit, policie, and ripe iudgement, as onelie act and counsell, with the losse of a verie few

of his companie, wrought all their safeties, which otherwise by treacherie had been most likelie to have beene intrapped.[49]

Sidney also became increasingly critical of his uncle's inept leadership and vainglorious shows, though his criticisms were necessarily muted. In a letter to the Earl of Leicester, he caustically recounted the "news in Roterdam,... that your band is of very hansome men, but meerly and unarmed spending monei and tyme to no purpos."[50] Later in the campaign he noted flaws in the overall strategy, complaining that instead of fortifying the "principal sea places" they already held, "we do still make camps and streight again mar them for want of meanes, and so lose our monei to no purpos." That same day he wrote Walsingham another guarded, but gloomy, assessment of their situation: "We are now four monthes behynd a thing unsupportable in this place. To complain of my Lord of Lester you know I mai not but ... I did never think our nation had been so apt to go to the Enemy as I fynd them."[51]

The skirmish at Zutphen, where Sidney received his fatal wound, provided an escape from these increasingly depressing strategic concerns. When the fog around the English camp lifted to reveal a large Spanish convoy, the English charged. Amidst the frustrations and delays of a prolonged siege campaign, the chance for hand-to-hand combat proved irresistible; the skirmish at Zutphen was, as Simon Adams says, a kind of "military catharsis."[52] The Earl of Leicester's report of the event and of his nephew's injuries betrays his own mixed feelings regarding the clash between the demands of honor and military discipline: "There was too many indeed at this skirmish of the better sort, but I was offended when I knew it, but could not fetch them back: but since they have all so well escaped (save my dear nephew), I would not for ten thousand pounds but they had been there since they have all won that honour they have."[53] Even the general entrusted with the responsibilities of command affirms the supremacy of honor. George Whetstone's poetic tribute renders the contradictions of Sidney's death even more poignant. Sir Philip's friend and mentor, Hubert Languet, had presciently warned him that "a man who falls at an early age cannot have done much for his country,"[54] and Whetstone's fallen Sidney laments his "inability to do my Countrey good":

> my service is but greene
> My yeares are young, and brought forth Leaves of late.
> The blomes were faire, but yet no fruit is seene,
> I studied have to benefit the state
> To execute I am forbid by fate.[55]

Yet Whetstone, a professional soldier who also fought at Zutphen, still concludes, as Leicester had, that the "lasting fame" secured by this exploit justifies the loss of Sidney's life.

Later accounts of Sidney's final battle become more romantically chivalric, adding legendary incidents of bravery and altruism. Fulke Greville's *Dedication* is the most powerfully hagiographic. In his version Sidney is wounded in the thigh because "the marshal of the camp [was] lightly armed," and Sidney's "unspotted emulation of his heart to venture without any inequality made him cast off his cuisses."[56] After he is shot, Sidney yields his cup of water to a dying foot soldier, uttering the immortal words, "Thy need is greater than mine."[57] Thomas Moffet says Sidney failed to arm himself adequately because he was hurrying to rescue a friend when he was slain by "a brigand's hand craftily hidden in a ditch."[58] He employs a trope of Renaissance chivalric romance extending from Ariosto's attack on gunpowder to Cervantes's lament that "a base and cowardly hand...[can] take the life of a brave knight."[59]

In many of these tributes the chivalric heroism of Sidney's death explicitly mutes the contradictions of his life, the clash between his own autonomy and ambition and his deference to the Queen. One writer says he died "of manly woundes receiued in seruice of his Prince...in the open fielde, in Martiall Maner, the honorablest death that could be desired, and best beseeming a Christian Knight, whereby he hath worthely wonne to him selfe immortal fame among the godly." From this point of view Sidney's life acquires a happy unity, reconciling heroic virility and dutiful obedience, activism and contemplation, as he passes smoothly "from the companie of the muses to the campe of Mars ... to followe the affayres of Chivalrie."[60] Fulke Greville's account of his friend's life is far more sophisticated, but it still imposes a balance between ambition and duty that is too pat. In Greville's biography Sidney's life finally presents an "exact image of quiet and action (happily united in him, and seldom well divided in any)."[61] In such elegiac tributes the chivalric compromise is imposed on the once volatile conflicts of Sidney's brief life. The "exact image of quiet and action" is, to some extent, a death mask of his own devising, an image perfectly embodied by the figure of "the Shepherd Knight." His fascination with the ceremonial surface of "the rites of knighthood" and his guilt about his own deeper ambitions kept him bound by that image in life and death.

After Sidney's death the figure of the Shepherd Knight endured in popular memory, celebrated in chivalric verse and ceremony. In a ballad by John Phillips, Sidney is recalled as a vapidly contented courtier:

> In Marshall feates I settled my delight,
> The stately steede I did bestride with ioy,
> At tilt and turney oft I tried my might,
> In these exploits I never felt annoy.[62]

In the 1590 Accession Day tilt Sir Henry Lee, the Lelius of the *New Arcadia*, retired as the Queen's champion in a ceremony conducted with great solemnity. To his successor, the Earl of Cumberland, he bequeathed a collection of his own tilt devices and poems from Sidney's *Old Arcadia*, a text Frances Yates calls "the scriptures of the perfect knight of Protestant chivalry." Sidney's posthumous image exemplifies the ironies of what Stephen Greenblatt calls "Renaissance self-fashioning," a process that often drastically diminishes "human autonomy in the construction of identity."[63]

Yet even here, at Lee's retirement tilt, a dissonant note intrudes. In George Peele's *Polyhymnia*, a versified record of the 1590 Accession Day tilt, the entry of the Earl of Essex is at least as dramatic as anyone else's. He appears "Yclad in mightie Armes of mourners hue" in honor of Sir Philip Sidney, "whose successor he / In Love and Armes had ever vowed to be."[64] According to Roy Strong, Essex would have been chosen as the Queen's champion had not his marriage to Frances Walsingham, Sidney's widow, come to light.[65] Instead of playing down the offense, Essex defiantly flaunts it, proclaiming his allegiance to Sidney and his new wife. In doing so, Essex sought to upstage the new champion by establishing a line of chivalric succession worthier and more heroic than that bequeathed by Lee and formally declaring himself its heir. As we shall see, the Earl of Essex claimed and exploited the Sidney legend for his own purposes, reawakening some of the contradictions behind it and transforming the "exact image of quiet and action" into a "dangerous image."

4

The Earl of Essex: "A Dangerous Image"

Robert Devereux, the second Earl of Essex, was Queen Elizabeth's most troublesome favorite. "No man was more ambitious of glory by vertue," writes William Camden, "no man more careless of all things else."[1] From its beginning his career was suffused with an aura of chivalric heroism. Essex was the stepson of Robert Dudley, the Earl of Leicester, and when Dudley embarked on his expedition to the Netherlands in 1585, Essex accompanied him as a general of the horse; the young Earl was only eighteen years old. No less extravagant than his stepfather, Essex spent a thousand pounds to outfit and equip his own force of seven hundred gentlemen and fifteen hundred common soldiers.[2] His grandfather, Sir William Knollys, objected strongly to such expenditures, warning that "wasteful prodigality hath devoured and will consume all noble men that be wilful in expenses."[3] Such exhortations were wasted on a young man confirmed in the traditional assumptions of aristocratic magnificence. Indeed, his ostentation was royally rewarded in 1588 at Tilbury, where Essex commanded a force of cavalry arrayed in the Devereux colors of white and tangerine.[4] According to Sir Henry Wotton, the young warrior outshone everyone, and the Queen "graced him openly in view of the Souldiers and people, even above my Lord of Leicester."[5]

Although he exulted in both, Essex enjoyed combat even more than "warlike shows." He was one of "the better sort" who could not resist plunging into the charge at Zutphen. After Sidney received his fatal injury, the fallen hero bequeathed his best sword to the young warrior, and Essex took on this chivalric legacy with reckless ardor. His youthful military exploits were marked by a bravado both dazzling and quixotic. In 1589, with the help of Roger Williams, he ran away to join Drake's expedition to Spain and Portugal. The Queen had already refused him permission, but he managed to elude her efforts to recall him. In Lisbon, as the rest of the English force withdrew, the Earl stayed behind to strike a heroic pose. According to one stirringly patriotic account, the "noble Essex in the courage of his Martiall bloud, ranne his speare and brake it against the Gates of that City: demanding alowde if any Spaniard mewed therein durst aduenture forth in fauour of his Mistresse to break a staffe with him. But those Gallants thought it safer to court their Ladies with amorous discourses, then to haue their loues written on their breasts with the point of his English Speare."[6] The challenge was not accepted, but the Earl's bravery won him enduring renown. Even after his death, the deed was celebrated in a ballad entitled "Essex's Last Goodnight," which recalls that

> The Portingals can witness be
> His Dagger at Lisbon gate he flung,
> And like a Knight of Chivalry,
> His chain upon the same he hung.[7]

On his return to England, Essex was forgiven by the Queen and greeted by George Peele's *Eclogue Gratulatorie*, which formally anointed him Sidney's chivalric heir:

> Fellow in Armes he was, in their flowing deies,
> With that great Shepherd good Philisides:
> And in sad sable did I see him dight
> Moning the misse of Pallas' peereles Knight.
>
> . . . .
>
> But, ah for griefe, that jolly groome is dead,
> For whom the Muses silver teares have shed:
> Yet in this lovelie swaine, source of our glee,
> Mun all his Vertues sweet reviven bee.[8]

The Earl's next chivalric adventure was treated less indulgently by his superiors. In 1591 he traveled to France to join forces with Henri IV. After his arrival Essex made a bold but pointless sortie across enemy territory, which ended with a splendid entry into the royal camp:

> As to the person of the said Earl of Essex...and those of his suite, nothing more magnificent could possibly be seen: for at his entry into Compiegne he had before him six pages mounted on chargers and dressed in orange velvet all embroidered with gold. And he himself had a military cloak...of orange velvet covered all with jewels. His saddle, bridle and the rest of his horse's harness were in like sort. His dress and the furniture of his horse alone were worth sixty thousand crowns. He had twelve tall body squires...and six trumpets sounding before him.[9]

Later in the campaign, after a long and futile siege of Rouen, Essex issued another challenge to personal combat to the governor of the city, which was also not accepted. These incidents prompted a stinging rebuke from the Privy Council, accusing him of first wasting time and money on a "privatt" and "unadvised jorney" while "leaving the armye without any head or martiall, and none else but a Serjeant Major," and then endangering his troops by making a "bravado uppon the enemy in the sight of the towne."[10] The reproach resembles the one delivered by Sidney's "olde governour," who rebukes Amphialus for seeking "rather...the glorie of a private fighter, than of a wise Generall" (*NA*, p. 414). The same conflict between military discipline and personal honor persists among "the better sort."

The pageants and spectacles of Elizabethan chivalry were supposed to resolve this conflict. The Earl of Essex was certainly an enthusiastic participant in "the rites of knighthood," and his appearances in the lists were frequent and flamboyant. In 1586 he was the second challenger in the Accession Day tilt, and the next year he led the challengers, riding out first against Sir Henry Lee and then against the Earl of Cumberland. In 1588 he began and ended the tilt, and in 1589 he led again. He ran three courses out of ten in 1593, and two out of nine in 1594, and he was the sole challenger in two additional tilts in 1594 and 1596. Several other young aristocrats aligned with the Essex faction were similarly drawn to chivalric combat. The

Earl of Bedford ran in ten tournaments from 1594 to 1600, and the Earl of Southampton entered eight times from 1593 to 1602, both men joining in the Essex revolt. The Earl of Sussex, who ran in ten tournaments from 1593 to 1602, was deeply implicated in the conspiracy, backing out only at the last minute. Charles Blount, Lord Mountjoy, a skilled performer in twelve tournaments from 1588 to 1599, was initially involved in secret contacts with James VI but broke away after replacing Essex as commander of the Irish campaign.[11] Sharing many of the same unruly ambitions, Essex and these other fractious young aristocrats were the most frequent participants in the Accession Day tilt during the last decade of Elizabeth's rule; loyalty to the Queen was probably a less compelling motive for them than their zeal for martial glory. Sir Henry Wotton found the Earl's chivalric shows far from innocent, and he condemned the "dangerous indiscretions of committing himself in his recreations and shooting matches to the publique view of so many thousand Citizens which usually flocked to see him, and made within the reach of his own ears large reclamations in his praise."[12]

Even in the tiltyard Essex was intent on winning praise and outshining the competition. He upstaged the Queen's official champion from the very start; in the 1590 Accession Day tilt, when George Clifford, the Earl of Cumberland, succeeded Sir Henry Lee, Essex appeared in mourning for Sir Philip Sidney, "whose successor he / In love and Armes had ever vowed to be."[13] Thus, he declared himself the heir to a worthier line of chivalric heroism. Cumberland was a loyal and moderate courtier, unattached to any faction, and these modest qualifications probably contributed to his selection as champion. Like Essex, he was also a military commander, but Clifford's privateering naval expeditions were quite profitable, whereas Essex returned from his more celebrated voyages empty-handed. Cumberland's military schemes were also less grandiose, a contrast evident in the planning for an attack on Spain in 1597. When both men submitted proposals to Burghley, the aged councillor characteristically preferred Cumberland's, calculating that if Essex's plan "shall not be taken in hand yet the Earl of Cumberland's offer might be taken without great charge and yet thereby offend the enemy."[14] No less characteristically, Burghley concluded these deliberations by adopting neither proposal. Cumberland must have cut an impressive figure in the tiltyard, on the evidence of his portraits by Nicholas Hilliard and the splendid suit of tilting armor preserved in the Metropolitan Museum of Art in New York. Nevertheless, for most of his time as champion Cumberland must have found himself "entirely overshadowed" by the more splendid Earl of Essex.[15]

Essex could finally endure no rivals anywhere, in battle or at court. In 1587, shortly after he returned to England from the Netherlands, he quarreled bitterly with Sir Walter Ralegh, petulantly demanding "whether I had cause to disdain his competition of Love, or whether I could have comfort to give myself over to the service of a Mistress that was in Awe of such a Man... I had no joy to be in any place, but loath to be near about her when I know my affection so much thrown down, and such a wretch as Ralegh highly esteemed of her."[16] Tournaments seemed to inflame Essex's competitive aggression instead of providing a cathartic release. Wotton recalls a "glorious feather-triumph, when he [Essex] caused two thousand orange-tawny Feathers in despight of Sr Walter Raleigh, to be worn in the Tilt-yard, even before her Majesties own face."[17] Such ostentatious shows were frequently competitive, but for Essex, the hostilities they expressed were constantly spilling over, beyond the bounds of the tiltyard. When Charles Blount flaunted a token awarded by Elizabeth for his skill at jousting—a gold queen from a chess set—Essex angrily remarked, "Now I perceive every fool must have a favour." Blount challenged Essex, and the latter was slightly injured in the duel that followed. The Queen may have been pleased with the outcome since she said she wanted someone to "take him [Essex] down and teach him better manners, otherwise there would be no rule with him."[18] However, Essex was no more mannerly or modest than before, since he succeeded in recruiting his former rival to his faction. Shortly after their duel Blount became the lover of the Earl's sister,

Penelope Devereux, and a friend of the Earl himself. Essex's hatred for those who remained his rivals persisted, to the growing annoyance of the Queen. One observer reported on the continuing rivalry of Essex and Ralegh, noting that "the disorder happened by my Lord of Essex has troubled her Majesty very much. He has challenged Sir Walter Ralegh, which is sought by the Council to be repressed and to be buried in silence that may not be known to her majesty."[19] William Camden saw this desire to surpass every rival as a fundamental flaw, one that finally poisoned his relationship with the Queen: "When now he had not onely an outward shew, but an inward power in the Queenes fauour, he made haste (as the wiser sort of the Courtiers complained) to outgoe both his equals and superiours, to detract from the praise of all which were not at his devotion, to frowne upon others which had any power or grace with the Queene, and by his courtesie and liberality to hunt after popular favour which is always of short continuance and unjust; and military praise, which is never but dangerous"; these shortcomings, combined with a "proud neglect of duty and observance...alienated the Queenes mind from him."[20]

No one was more sensitive to the risks of such impulses than Essex's adviser, Francis Bacon, particularly since Bacon's career had suffered from the effects of his patron's vaunting ambitions. Essex had pressed hard to place his own candidates in high government positions, but Bacon was finally denied the posts of Attorney General and Solicitor General in 1594. Bacon's earlier opposition to the government's position in the Parliament of 1593 did not help his candidacy, but neither did his patron's aggressive partisanship. By 1595 Bacon was determined to rectify these errors and heal the divisions between Essex and the Queen, and he shrewdly chose the occasion of the Accession Day tilt to accomplish these purposes, knowing the importance of the event for both Essex and the Queen. He also understood its ritual function as a means of mediating conflict. However, before publicly undertaking these delicate negotiations, Bacon wrote privately to William Cecil to communicate his own position. He assured the Queen's senior adviser that he would not "divide myself between her Majesty and the causes of other men (as others have done) but ... attend her business only."[21] He justified his parliamentary opposition of 1593 with an intriguing rationalization, which, even if it were not entirely convincing, still accorded with a commonplace Renaissance trope. Bacon contended that in fact he spoke first for the government position, "and that which I after spake in difference was but in circumstances of time and manner, which methinks should be no great matter, since there is variety allowed in counsel, as a discord in music, to make it more perfect" (*Works*, 8:362). He concludes by promising Burghley that henceforward "your Lordship shall bestow your benefit upon one that hath more sense of obligation than of self-love" (8:363).

Bacon subsequently composed a masque of Love and Self-Love for the 1595 Accession Day tilt, dramatizing the shrewd sophistries of his letter in the flattering euphemisms of courtly allegory. In this context his earlier efforts at self-serving ingratiation are incorporated within a larger, more high-minded design—the "chivalrous design" of Elizabethan pageantry. Had the design worked, Bacon might have succeeded in advancing his own aims while serving both his mistress and his master, reconciling their conflicts through a deft *discordia concors*. Unfortunately, the device was both a formal and a practical failure.

The masque of Love and Self-Love used the Accession Day tournament to dramatize the skills and the predicament of the Earl of Essex. In the fragments of the device that remain, the Earl appears as the young knight Erophilus, or Love. He is addressed by the three orators of Philautia, or Self-Love: a Hermit, a Soldier, and a Statesman. The orators all praise Essex for his great talents in each field, and they encourage him to apply them for his own advancement. Each proclaims the selfish advantage of his own calling while deriding the disadvantages of love. The Hermit emphasizes the thanklessness of such devotion while praising a life of contemplation:

> Will he never cease to profess that is not believed, to offer that is not accepted, and tax himself at that which is not remitted? Doth he not perceive that the infiniteness of the affection

which he pretendeth and the obligation which he acknowledgeth doth but diminish the thanks of his services.

(*Works* 8:378)

After each speaker has made his appeal, Bacon shows, in the terms of his letter to Burghley, how he can coordinate their "variety in counsel, as a discord in music to make it more perfect." Although Erophilus remains steadfast against the allure of Self-Love, he resolves his predicament by pursuing all three courses. He can thus apply his many talents not for his own advantage but for the service of the Queen:

For her recreation, he will confer with his muse: for her defence and honour, he will sacrifice his life in the wars, hoping to be embalmed in the sweet odours of her remembrance; to her service will he consecrate all his watchful endeavours; and will ever bear in his heart the picture of her beauty, in his actions of her will, and in his fortune of her grace and favour.

(8:386)

The final chord was not, unfortunately, the anticipated *discordia concors*; it was, instead, distinctly discordant. Following the formal proclamation of Erophilus's devotion, the Queen abruptly rose and said "that if she had thought their had bene so moch said of her, she wold not haue been their that Night, and soe went to Bed."[22] Elizabeth may have been bored or fatigued, but her frequently incongruous reactions to courtly performance were usually more deliberate than capricious. They suggest a determined resistance to rhetorical manipulation, however ingratiating its blandishments. Here too she effectively shattered the illusion of harmonious dialogue, just as she had with the *Lady of May*, by forcibly reminding performers and spectators that she was in charge and had the last word. Bacon had tried to achieve a compromise solution, which acknowledged the Queen's supremacy while promoting his patron's virtues and greatness before the entire court. He was also trying to project a more balanced image of Essex, one that combined chivalric aggression with more peaceful activities and professions of loyal service. Yet the show was ultimately, as Roy Strong says, "an extravagant flop."[23] The chivalric compromise was beginning to fail.

To Bacon's horror, the Earl's overweening military ambitions only increased after this incident, further upsetting the balance Bacon had tried to strike in his Accession Day device. In 1596 the Earl led an expedition to Cadiz. The command was actually divided between Essex and the Lord Admiral, and despite dramatic victories over the Spanish fleet, the effectiveness of the campaign was hampered by their competition. During the attack on Cadiz the Spanish gained time to burn the ships they could not defend while the English galleons struggled to "jockey each other out of the fighting line."[24] Thus, the English were deprived of considerable plunder, and since this had been one of the expedition's main objectives, the Queen was angry with the loss. She was also annoyed with the large number of knighthoods Essex conferred on those who fought with him since she regarded these honors as her own to bestow. By knighting men in battle, Essex established an almost feudal bond of loyalty to himself, and Elizabeth resented this military encroachment on the allegiance of her subjects.

After the battle the conflicts continued back in England as Essex and his cohorts sought to promote their version of events. Fearing that the Lord Admiral's "sea faction do seek to disgrace my lord's noble actions," Essex's agents tried to publish a report called *The True Relation of the Action at Cadiz* before the Earl returned, but the government discovered their schemes and suppressed its publication. Anthony Bacon still arranged for foreign circulation of manuscript copies, and one of the Earl's chaplains preached a sermon at Paul's Cross, comparing the Earl "with the chiefest generals" and declaring that "honour and valour will flourish, maugre malice and envy itself."[25]

In 1597 the Earl commanded an expedition to the Azores, but the voyage was again marred by envy and competition. When Sir Walter Ralegh set out to reconnoiter one of the islands, Essex ordered him back lest Ralegh win the honor of going ashore first. With a rashness reminiscent of Sidney's, Essex then leapt with only his sword and collar into a boat rowed by men no more adequately armed. When Ralegh yelled to warn him that he should take his helmet and breastplate since there were musketeers on shore, Essex replied that "he disdained to take any advantage of the watermen that rowed him."[26]

Essex returned from these expeditions with a firm resolve. He was determined to secure preeminence over his rivals in both the rights and the "rites" of knighthood by acquiring the post of Earl Marshal. The post had been held by a commission since the death of the Earl of Shrewsbury in 1590, but Essex wanted it for himself. His military ambitions gravely alarmed Francis Bacon, who wrote a letter in October 1596 outlining the difficulties of his patron's position. The Earl was a "man of a nature not to be ruled; of an estate not grounded to his greatness; of a popular reputation; of a military dependence: I demand whether there can be a more dangerous image than this represented to any monarch living, much more to a lady, and of her Majesty's apprehensions?" (*Works*, 9:41). Bacon advised Essex to seek a civil rather than military office, conceding that the Earl might retain his martial greatness "in substance" but insisting that he "abolish it in shows" to the Queen (9:43). The problem with this advice was that a noble reputation depended as much on public performance and display as on greatness in substance, and Essex could never settle for substance alone.[27]

Essex completely ignored Bacon's advice and pursued the earl marshalcy with fierce determination. After returning from the Azores expeditions, he withdrew from court and refused to return until the office was bestowed. Even when he finally obtained it, he sought to aggravate, rather than mute, the "dangerous image" it presented. Robert Cecil drew up a patent of office based on the Earl of Shrewsbury's and sent it to Essex for review. The Earl arrogantly returned it to Cecil, demanding that it be rewritten: "I send you back this paper in which I have been bold to make a note or two, and especially have underlined some lines where I am praised for too innocent virtues, where they are active virtues and not negative that should draw on a prince to bestow a marshal's office."[28] The draft of the letters patent is among the Cecil manuscripts at Hatfield House, and the virtues Essex underlined are indeed rather bland: "*bene, iuste, pie, ac decente & salutariter praesunt*": "they preside well, justly, piously, and decently and advantageously."[29]

In his letter Essex touches glancingly on one of the fundamental contradictions at the heart of aristocratic status: the latent conflict between inherent distinction and that bestowed by the monarch—"native" and "dative" honor. Here he insists that his own active virtues precede and determine the honors given by the monarch. As Earl Marshal he developed the point still further in a speech delivered during a trial at Essex House in 1599 regarding rival claims to a barony. Initially conceding that "all nobility is from the prince," he still insists that the sovereign is bound by certain conditions: "God hath tied himself to the honor of men, and so should the prince do likewise." Essex spells out these conditions with some precision, arguing that "the favor of princes should be regular," "the upholding of nobility is a most necessary and a religious care," the nobility "are the very subaltern parts of the prince," and, finally, England was "most mighty when the nobility led and commanded in war and were great housekeepers at home."[30]

Essex's motives for wanting to be Earl Marshal were complex. He wanted first of all to secure precedence over all his rivals, especially Charles Howard, the Lord Admiral. The latter's recent creation as Earl of Nottingham and Lord Steward irritated Essex for two reasons: the latter had to yield to Howard on state occasions, and in Essex's view, Nottingham's letters patent glorified the Lord Admiral's role at Cadiz by slighting his own.[31] His anger erupted in a letter to the Queen complaining of her failure to "have the injurious letters patent altered" after she had promised to do so.[32] Unhappy at this point both with his own letters patent and their praise for "too innocent virtues" and with those of the Earl of Nottingham, Essex put all blame on his rival. He accuses him of obstructing the desired changes in one or the other and contends that "the stop was *non quia fremuere gentes* [not because the people complained], but because one man only stormed at it." Essex first proposes to prove his claims by introducing officers from the campaign as witnesses to his own superiority. Perhaps remembering Bacon's admonition, he professes to do this in deference to her majesty's preference for "civil proof." Yet he cannot resist settling things his own way, so he also offers to challenge Nottingham or any of his adherents in the conviction that "when I shall be with any such champion apart, I shall quickly bring him to your Majesty *consitentem* [*sic*] *reum* [a confessing defendant or criminal]."[33] Elizabeth tried to resolve this conflict with a characteristic compromise. Nottingham's letters patent remained unchanged, leaving his honors intact, while Essex was created Earl Marshal without any known changes in his. Indeed, no record, except the draft, of Essex's creation as Earl Marshal survives, and the controversy surrounding his appointment may have prevented its official enrollment.[34] Nevertheless, despite the Queen's efforts to strike a balance of honors allotting "favour sufficient" to each rival, the chivalric compromise failed again. Essex was clearly the victor, and Nottingham resigned his steward's rod and withdrew from court, pretending to be sick.[35] The victory was an important one because more was at stake than ceremonial honors.

In his ardent campaign for this office Essex was driven by a desire for more than precedence or even supreme military authority. As Earl Marshal he would preside over the court's stately and chivalric ceremonies as well as the Court of Chivalry; he would also be a kind of commander in chief.[36] However, as his speech in praise of nobility indicates, he was determined to revive the customary rights behind "the rites of knighthood" and claim for the highest surviving feudal office a "subaltern," constitutional authority. As soon as he became Earl Marshal, he initiated extensive research on the status and privileges of the office, evidently determined to make full use of all its powers. The broad scope of these inquiries is suggested by the large number of correspondents involved in it. Francis Thynne, the Lancaster herald, prepared a treatise on the Earl's illustrious predecessors, which asserted that the "office of the erle marshall" has such "antiquity, honor, and credit" that "fewe other offices eyther for place or dignitye are preferred before yt eyther amongst us or forraine nationes."[37] Augustine Vincent, a clerk in the Tower record office, drew up a list touching "the summary points of all that I and others found concerning the office of Earle Marshall, when wee were commanded by the Earle of Essex Earl Marshall to make search in the records for the same 1597." An endnote indicates that he passed it on to a successor twenty years later: "This I delivered to the Earle of Arundel 1617."[38] Even Lord Henry Howard joined the search, "rifling all corners of my dusty cabinet about notes belonging to an honour, that doth now concern youself,... that I may rightly judge, and you may truly understand what is due to your authority."[39] The result of his labors is a lengthy manuscript treatise promoting the conservative reforms attempted by his brother, the Duke of Norfolk, in 1568, for Lord Henry also opposes the granting of arms "wthout the warrant of an Earle Marshal" and rails against abuses by individual heralds.[40] Howard makes a strong case in his "Brief Discourse on the Right Use of Giving Arms" for the Earl Marshal's supreme authority on "all questions of honor," refuting those who would argue "that the Sou[er]aigne is only absolut, for therein all records agree, because it is well said by civilians, that *Princeps uidetur facere cum dat aucthoritatem faciendi* [the prince seems to make when he gives authority of making]."[41]

The most intriguing response is a fragmentary, anonymous tract among the Cotton manuscripts. It begins with a declaration of the writer's zeal and industry, couched in tones of humble deference:

> While I was ernestly in hand with this labour, searching cifting posting upp and downe to frends and antiquaries sorting and comparing whatsoever diligent enquirie with unwearied affection was able to congest rather out of fragments scattered then certaine rules recorded in that forme y[e]t I coulde wishe touching the Marshalls Jurisdiction his liberties his privileges his services his fees his iudgement in all pointes of honor his commaundimet over Heralds his direction of combates etc. I was giuen to understand that your Lo: had directed all the notes about this subject that weare sent to you from many frendes to the distribution and disposition of one learned frend much better able then my selfe to marshall thinges so long putt out of course in a certen forme.[42]

Before it breaks off, the treatise advances an extremely audacious proposal: it first advocates that the position of Earl Marshal should be formally combined with that of the lapsed office of Constable and then argues that Essex is entitled by descent, as well as virtue, to the office of Constable "whensoever it shall please her Highnes to restore to bloode what in former tymes was houlden dew to posterity."[43] By reviving the vacant office and awarding it to Essex, Elizabeth would have formally unified the jurisdiction of the Court of Chivalry. Twenty-five years later King James did just that when, persuaded by the precedents presented by another antiquary, Sir Robert Cotton, he bestowed both titles on the Earl of Arundel. The earlier treatise, prepared for the Earl of Essex, makes a very strong case for combining these "chiefe offices of this Realme" and another already held by Essex, "the Grand Esquier or Mr. of the horse," by comparing the combination with the Trinity, citing "that maxime of the Holy Ghost, *funiculus triplex no[n] facile rumpitur* [a triple cord is not easily broken]." The Queen would thus resolve the "many questions and scruples [that] have arisen heretofore about the proportions of difference betwene the chardges of the Marshall and the Constable together with their entercommuning."[44] What the tract does not point out are the risks to the sovereign of conferring both these offices on a man as ambitious as Essex.

The earl marshalcy presented a sufficiently "dangerous image" in Bacon's view, but the threats posed by the Constable were even graver. Another antiquary, Francis Legh, spells them out in his discourse on "The Antiquity and Office of the Constable of England." He says that "the greatness of these officers hath bin a cause of much trouble to their princes in France," adding, "We haue not bin free in England from tumults raysed by these great officers." Elizabeth's father, Henry VIII, executed his Constable, Edward Stafford, the Duke of Buckingham, and left the office vacant because, Legh writes, "it was high and dangerous." Legh records the opinion that "the constable of England by virtue of his office may arrest the king," only to dismiss such an opinion as "an idle tradition."[45] Nevertheless, it remained a durable, if somewhat dormant, idea, kept alive throughout the sixteenth century. The Steward and Constable had led the barons' revolt against Edward II, and their opposition was justified in principle in the *Modus Tenendi Parliamentum*, the tract bound together with the *Treatises on the Earl Marshal of England* in the volumes owned by the Duke of Norfolk and the Earl of Leicester.

Earlier in the sixteenth century there were two significant political treatises that set out to incorporate the high feudal offices of Constable, Steward, and Earl Marshal into a system of mixed government that could oppose royal tyranny. Thomas F. Mayer has argued that Thomas Starkey's *Dialogue Between Reginald Pole and Thomas Lupset* is "one of the most significant works of political thought written in English between Fortescue and Hooker," combining Venetian republican ideals with ancient feudal institutions in "an aristocratic reform manifesto."[46] Invoking the older native tradition, Starkey asserts that "our old ancestors, the institutors of our laws and order of our realm considering well this same tyranny, and for the avoiding of the same, ordained a Constable of England, to counterpoise the authority of the prince and temper the same—giving him authority to call a parliament in such case as the prince would run into any tyranny of his own heady judgement." Starkey concedes the dangers of such an "over-high" post and notes its recent suppression, but he argues that it will be "much more convenient...to give this authority unto diverse and not to one." In an emergency, the Constable could summon and head a counsel or "little parliament" consisting of the Marshal, Steward, and Chamberlain, plus representatives of the judges, citizens, and bishops, "to redress the affects of the prince to the order of the law, justice and equity."[47] John Ponet, a Marian exile, makes a similar argument in his *Short Treatise of Politic Power*, recalling "the memorie of the auncient office of the highe Constable of Englande, vnto whose autoritie it perteined, ont [not] only to summone the king personally before the parliament or other courtes of iudgement (to anser and receaue according to iustice) but also vpon iuste occasion to committe him vnto warde."[48] In both these earlier Tudor works one can see the same ideological conversion of feudal status into constitutional authority—an effort that occasionally succeeded. John Guy and David Starkey have shown how the aristocracy's overthrow of Thomas Cromwell in 1540 and recovery of preeminence in the Privy Council were motivated, in part, by ideas of their ancient privileges.[49]

The research initiated by Essex is thus another "missing link" between earlier medieval and Tudor theories of mixed government and the parliamentary opposition of the seventeenth century. In the case discussed by David Starkey the connection is a manuscript volume of the *Modus Tenendi Parliamentum* owned first by the Earl Marshal, the Duke of Norfolk, and subsequently by the parliamentarian, Edward Coke. Here the link is the research undertaken by the College of Heralds and the Society of Antiquaries. From Thomas Starkey through the antiquaries to Coke there is a shared interest in the great feudal offices and a shared belief in the superiority of mixed government.

In the seventeenth century the antiquarian's research on feudal offices and institutions became increasingly controversial. Sir Robert Cotton, for one, found that while his work on the royal pedigree and older means of raising revenues met with the approval of King James, research on parliament and its precedents did not. Discourses on the antiquity and offices of Constable, Marshal, and Steward were probably less inflammatory, but they still upheld principles of mixed government, assigning authority to the nobility as well as the King. As James Farnell explains, the Society of Antiquaries was not perceived in its own time as "a group of dull, harmless pedants" but rather as "historical revolutionaries," whose research challenged royal prerogative and provoked growing government suspicion.[50] When in 1607 Cotton tried to secure royal patronage for an antiquarian academy, he failed. Richard Carew maintained that "they were obliged to dissolve themselves and break their Society lest ... they should be prosecuted as a Cabal against the Government."[51] Cotton continued his researches, becoming gradually estranged from the government. By 1629, after he had aligned himself with the parliamentary opposition, he was arrested, and by government order his magnificent library was sealed, its books deemed a source of sedition. The fragmentary treatise addressed to Essex in 1597 proposes to combine the jurisdiction of two high feudal offices, a scheme Cotton would later successfully promote. The proposal is not explicitly revolutionary, but the revival of the office of Constable reestablishes an authority potentially capable of challenging royal sovereignty.

Bolstered by his newly acquired authority as Earl Marshal, Essex himself became increasingly recalcitrant. In 1598 he and the Queen argued bitterly over the appointment of a Lord Governor of Ireland. When the quarrel grew so heated that he turned his back on her, Elizabeth boxed his ears. Essex reached for his sword, and after he was restrained by the others around them, he stormed from the room. In their efforts to resolve this crisis, his elders all urged humble submission. Sir Thomas Egerton told him that between monarch and subject "there can be no proportion of duty"; Sir Francis Knollys said that "there is no contesting between sovereignty and obedience"; and Sir Henry Lee wrote that "your honor is more dear to you than your life, yet consider that she is your sovereign, whom you may not treat upon equal conditions."[52] All make the same point, a basic tenet of Tudor orthodoxy: no "proportion" is possible in the relation between subject and sovereign when their interests really conflict, and obedience is the only solution. The only feasible compromise was the one proposed by Elizabeth to Leicester when their interests clashed. Thinking it "a hard bargain when both parties are losers," she allowed a balance of honors, one that Leicester accepted. Unfortunately, Essex was, as Wotton says, "no good Pupill to my Lord of Leicester," and the favors that sufficed for his stepfather would never satisfy him.[53]

Essex was determined to remake the chivalric compromise on his own terms. In his view there had to be a "proportion" between the Queen and her powerful subjects that would constitute a balance of power as well as honors. He wrote to Egerton, the cautious Lord Keeper, demanding, "Cannot Princes erre? Can they not wrong their Subiects? Is any earthly power infinite? Pardon me, pardon me, my good Lord, I can never subscribe to these principles." Instead, he boldly proclaimed his own principles, beginning with Sidney's belief in

the subject's "native and legal freedom" and advancing to the
more exalted rights of noble status and feudal office: "What I
owe as a Subiect I know, and what as an Earle, and Marshall of
England: to serve as a servant and a slave I know not."[54]

Essex still found it almost impossible to act on these principles, just as Sidney had before him. He also found it hard to
enact the lofty military role he obtained. When he acquired the
command of the Irish expedition, he led forth an immense
army consisting of sixteen thousand foot soldiers and thirteen
hundred cavalry.[55] Nevertheless, he took on the assignment
with deep misgivings. Just before departing in 1599 he wrote
that "I am not ignorant what are the disadvantages of absence,
the opportunities of practicing enemies, when they are neither
encountered nor overlooked, the constructions of Princes
under whom *magna fama* is more dangerous than *mala*." For
Essex, his "dangerous image" was losing its savor, but its obliga-
tions were still inescapable: he had to go because "I am tied to
my own reputation to use not tergiversation."[56] Once in Ireland,
Essex conducted a weak and ineffective compaign, noteworthy
only for the large number of knighthoods he conferred, equal
to a quarter of the number of knights in England.[57] He concluded it by returning to England against orders on September
28 and barging unannounced into the Queen's bedroom. Essex
effectively destroyed himself by this last excess, and Elizabeth
never saw him again. He was promptly arrested, charged with
insubordination, and confined within his own house for nearly
a year.

An incident that occurred during that year demonstrated
just how dangerous his "dangerous image" had become. Early
in 1600 an engraving began circulating that caused a sensation
at court and in the city. Rowland Whyte reported that "some
foolish idle headed ballad maker of late cawsed many of his
[Essex's] pictures to be printed on horsback, with all his titles of
honor, all his services, and two verses underneath that gave
hym exceeding praise for wisdom, honor, worth; that heaven
and earth approve yt, Gods elected."[58] The original engraving
had been made by Thomas Cockson probably before the Earl's
departure for Ireland in anticipation of his success there; it

7. Thomas Cockson's engraving of the Earl of Essex on horseback (by permission of the Folger Shakespeare Library).

showed his previous military exploits in the foreground and on the sides—Rouen, Cadiz, and the Azores—with Ireland looming ahead on the horizon, awaiting his triumphant arrival (Figure 7). Cockson had also done similar equestrian engravings of three other Earls.[59] Despite the disappointment of these high hopes for the Irish campaign, the Earl of Essex remained enormously popular in London, and the engraving was reprinted and sold. While under house arrest the Earl disappeared from the public eye, but this engraving kept his heroic martial image in circulation and sustained his popular reputation. The Privy Council was apparently troubled by the sale of this picture and acted that summer to suppress it. Its action was significantly categorical, including a whole class of illustrations such as the series done by Cockson:

> There is of late a use brought up to engrave in brasse the pictures of noblemen and other persons and then to sell them printed in paper sett forth oftentimes with verses and other circumstances not fytte to be used. Because this custome doth growe common and indeed is not meete such publique setting forth of anie pictures but of her most excellent Majesty should be permytted yf the same be well done, wee have for divers good respects thought good to praie your Grace [the Archbishop of Canterbury] that you will give direccion that hereafter no personage of any noblemann or other person shalbe ingraven and printed to be putt to sale publiquely, and those prints that are already made to be called in, unless your Lordship shall first be made acquainted with the same, and thincke meete to allow them.[60]

The blanket suppression of "anie pictures but of her most excellent Majesty" shows how the pressures of Elizabethan politics led to the breakdown of the Elizabethan courtly esthetic. For most of her reign, as Roy Strong says, "Elizabeth had no need to draw men's eyes to contemplate her," and the multiple focus of Elizabethan chivalry allowed considerable freedom and flexibility. By 1600, however, the Queen found it much harder to share the stage with her powerful nobles because their aggressive aspirations were increasingly insubordinate.

The collapse of the chivalric compromise is clearly manifest in the tensions surrounding the 1600 Accession Day tilt. In the late summer of that year Essex was finally released from his confinement. He was eager to have the sweet-wines monopoly—the source of his lavish income for the last decade—renewed, but this was denied him in October. He also hoped to regain access to the Queen, and once again the

Accession Day tilt seemed the appropriate occasion for negotiating this rapprochement. The space allotted to an "Unknown Knight" was reserved for Essex, according to Strong, but his friends' efforts to include him in the festivities ultimately failed.[61] He marked the occasion with a poignant letter: "Vouchsafe, dread sovereign, to know there lives a man, tho' dead to the world, that doth more true honour to your thrice blessed day, than all those, that appear in your fight." Privation has made him aware of his own dependence at least for the moment, teaching a humble devotion never experienced amidst the exhilarating splendors of the tiltyard: "For they which feel the comfortable influence of your favour or stand in the bright beams of your presence, rejoice partly for your Majesty's, but partly for their own happiness. Only miserable Essex, full of pain, full of sickness, full of sorrow, languishing in repentance for his offences past ... joys only for your Majesty's great happiness and happy greatness."[62]

Despite his professed repentance, Essex was excluded from the Accession Day tilt. Elizabeth and her advisers were undoubtedly loath to renew contact, but they were also probably resolved to prevent the popular Earl's reappearance as an "Unknown Knight" before the court and people of London. The simple equestrian engraving had already proved a sufficiently "dangerous image," and the Earl himself, armed and on horseback, could no longer be accommodated within the ceremonial confines of the tiltyard. Moreover, even more docile courtiers were becoming troublesome. Rowland Whyte had written the month before that "this yeare her Majesty wold have very great care taken that her coronacion day be with gallant solemnyties at tilt and turney observed, to the end the embassador of Russia may hold yt in admiracion."[63] Yet the tilt began with a speech by the Earl of Cumberland as a "Discontented Knight." Because the Earl was aggrieved about losing the governorship of the Isle of Wight, he complained that his loyal service had earned him no reward.[64] By the end of her reign the Queen's own champion had to be "forced to joust."[65]

On February 8, 1602, the Earl of Essex led several "Discontented Knights" in a confused and disorderly rebellion, which was easily and swiftly suppressed. His motives were in some ways almost as confusing as his strategy. The loss of his income was certainly a severe blow, and his hatred of his enemies at court also drove him to desperate measures. Lacy Baldwin Smith suggests he was clinically paranoid, and the Earl's erratic behavior throughout his attempted coup and afterward render doubts about his sanity legitimate.[66] Nevertheless, there were also serious ideological principles behind his rebellion even if he finally failed as their spokesman. As Earl Marshal, Essex regarded himself as both defender of the honor code and leader of "the flower of the nobility and gentry of England," as Mervyn James has shown; the Earl saw his revolt as a necessary attempt to purge the realm of "base upstarts."[67] When asked during his imprisonment what authority he had for undertaking to "remove such evils, as the commonwealth is burthened with," he replied "that he was earl marshal of England, and needed no other warrant."[68] Finally, if he read and pondered the results of the research he initiated on this high feudal office and sought to combine its jurisdiction with the Constable's, he might have felt himself authorized to broker the succession.

Essex was, in fact, accused of harboring such designs by one of his enemies sometime later. After Essex's execution Henry Percy, Earl of Northumberland, wrote King James that although Essex was a man "endeued wyth good gifts, yet was his losse the happiast chance for yowr maiestie and england that cowld befawle ws" because the late Earl could not "dreame of any thinge but hawing the continowall pouar of ane army to dispose of, of being great constable of england, to the end that in an interregnum he might call parlaments to make laws for owr selwes. Did he not decree it, that it was scandalus to owr nation that a stranger sould be owr king? ... Did hes soldiers followars dreme or speake any thing but of hes being king of england?"[69] The charges are wild and at some points patently false. Far from opposing James as a stranger king, Essex began negotiations, as Cecil and others did, to facilitate James's succession and ingratiate himself with the new sovereign. Yet, as these negotiations indicate, he was eager to have a role in settling the succession, and the authority of Earl Marshal and Constable gave that role greater legitimacy. Robert Parsons slyly attributed such ambitions to him as early as 1595 by anonymously dedicating *A Conference About the Next Succession to the Crown of England* to Essex: "No man is in more high & eminent place or dignitie at this day in our realme, then your selfe, whether we respect your nobilitie, or calling, or fauour with your prince, or high liking of the people, & consequently no man like to haue a greater part or sway in deciding of this great affaire."[70]

The Earl's revolt was finally a failure, ending in his arrest and execution. Nevertheless, it still did lasting damage, destroying the court's factional balance of power. For forty years the Queen had maintained a kind of political equilibrium by insuring that, as Robert Lacey explains, "no single man or group of men should have exclusive control over office, patronage or access to her presence."[71] Essex would not settle for this compromise solution. Driven by his ambition for preeminence, he gradually destroyed both himself and the system. Ironically, he forced Elizabeth to fall back on his hated rival, Robert Cecil. Her reaction established "the pattern of a single chief minister which she had fought so hard to avoid, and which was to be, through Cecil himself, Buckingham and Strafford, one of the most prominent and hated characteristics of the early Stuart autocracy."[72]

The Essex rebellion also destroyed the Elizabethan chivalric compromise. For most of her reign chivalric spectacle had sustained a ceremonial equilibrium, allowing a large number of contestants to participate in symbolic combat. The ritual aim was the achievement of a vigorous *discordia concors*, expressing and occasionally reconciling the conflicting impulses of the participants. The banishment of Essex from the lists and the bitter complaints of the Queen's own champion in the 1600 Accession Day tilt show how this compromise was failing; the revolt finished it off. Its destruction was powerfully dramatized by the play selected by the conspirators. Shakespeare's *Richard II* evidently was chosen for its deposition scene, but the play's opening depicts a more insidious loss of power. Richard II initially is confident in his own sovereignty. Nevertheless, he finds himself unable to preside over "the chivalrous design of knightly trial" because of his own guilty implication in its cause. He must therefore break it off. No longer containable within "the chivalrous design," the conflict explodes into revolution engulfing and destroying the monarch himself. The failure of judicial combat weakens the entire realm because it drains away the ruler's legitimacy. Elizabeth survived the Essex rebellion but died not long afterward. Her court's complex system of political and ceremonial balance, its own "chivalrous design," was shattered.

5

Samuel Daniel:
"The Voyce of Present Times"

The Earl of Essex inspired many writers both before and after
his death, but one of his most ardent admirers was the poet
Samuel Daniel. In the first edition of *The Civil Wars*, published in 1595, Daniel praised both Essex and Charles Blount,
Lord Mountjoy, as the incarnation of contemporary chivalric
heroism:

> You in whose actions yet the image shines
> Of ancient honor neere worne out of date,
> You that haue vertue into fashion brought
> In these neglected times respected nought.[1]

Blount was Daniel's patron, and the poet says that Blount could
reduce "Whole landes and Provinces" to "calme obedience"
(*CW*, p. 312). But his praise for Essex is more high-flown: the
Earl could lead a second crusade "Against the strength of all
the Eastern Powres":

> Thence might thy valor haue brought in despight
> Eternall Tropheis to Elizas name,
> And laid downe at her sacred feete the right
> Of all thy deedes and glory of the same.
> All that which by her powre, and by thy might
> Thou hadst attaind to her immortall fame
> Had made thee wondred here, admir'd a farre
> The Mercury of peace, the Mars of warre.
>   (pp. 311–312)

Daniel's vision of the chivalric compromise combines courtly
eloquence with military might through a comparison frequently
employed by Elizabethan courtiers: George Gascoigne's per-

sonal motto was *"Tam Marti quam Mercurio"*—"As [devoted] to Mars as Mercury."[2] Francis Bacon projected the same hopeful synthesis in his Accession Day masque of 1595—a synthesis disrupted by the Queen's abrupt departure.

Daniel's vision of chivalric harmony was also marred by events, the first of these being the civil wars he describes. The poem explicitly acknowledges the disruptive encroachment of past misfortunes on its "great designes" (*CW*, p. 312). If the blood shed in "thirteene battels fought / About this quarrel, fatall to our land" had only been "reseru'd with glory to haue brought / Nations and Kingdomes vnder our command," then English heroism might have triumphed throughout the world (pp. 310–311). The heirs of Henry V might have retained control of France, and Henry VIII could have extended his dominion to encompass the entire "Western Empire" (p. 311). With Elizabeth securely established as Henry VIII's "imperial daughter" and "Th'admired glorie of the earth," and with "proud Iberus lord" confined to Spain's "barraine boundes," even greater glories could have been won by Essex and his cohorts in Daniel's own time, epic victories the poet would gladly have celebrated (p. 311). Unfortunately, these are merely thoughts "Of what might haue beene" (p. 312). Since the "acted mischiefes [of the civil wars] cannot be vnwrought," Daniel must cease contemplating the "imagined good" of his chivalric vision and return to the sordid crimes of actual history (p. 312).

Daniel's imaginary triumph of Elizabethan chivalry was further disrupted by the misdeeds of his own time, in ways he did not anticipate. Instead of winning "Eternall Trophies to Elizas name," the Earl of Essex revolted against her rule. Within a few years the Earl's "image ... of ancient honor" had become as dangerous an image as the engraving of Essex on horseback, and Daniel therefore omitted the stanzas praising Essex from the 1601 edition. Following Blount's fall from favor and subsequent death, he removed the entire section from the 1609 edition of *The Civil Wars*.[3]

The difficulties of this passage are typical of Daniel's work as a whole. The chivalric compromise is shattered by the civil wars of the past and, still more dramatically, by the tumults and conspiracies of the present. Daniel was shocked by the Essex revolt, yet his reaction was profoundly ambivalent. Although he suppressed the stanzas praising Essex, he later addressed a verse epistle to a fellow conspirator, celebrating the Earl of Southampton's release from prison while comparing him to Cato, the noble opponent of Caesar's tyranny and paragon of republican virtue. He also wrote a play, *Philotas*, which many regarded as a defense of Essex, and he had to appear before the Privy Council to answer these suspicions. Despite his declared allegiance to authority and order, Daniel admired the noble rebel, and he could not decide which side he favored. Despite his praise for peace, he was fascinated by the energies unleashed by war, and he could not decide which of their virtues he preferred—order or honor.

In Daniel's case the literary text proved as vulnerable to the contradictions it sought to mediate as the social texts of Elizabethan chivalry. Indeed, these contradictions eventually overwhelmed his most ambitious undertakings and prevented their completion. Daniel's narrative breaks down, in the way described by Fredric Jameson in *The Political Unconscious*, as his "entire system of ideological closure [becomes]...the symptomatic projection of something quite different, namely of social contradiction."[4] In *The Civil Wars* Daniel set out to write an epic account of England's turbulent history from the reign of Richard II down to the beginning of the Tudor dynasty under Henry VII. Despite sustained and recurrent efforts to complete the poem, Daniel failed to do so, ending it with the reign of Edward IV. A second attempt in prose, *The Collection of the History of England*, was even more ambitious, beginning with a brief account of Roman rule and proposing to include a survey of the reigns of the "fiue Soueraigne Princes of the Line of Tewdor," but it too fell short of the goal, ending with the reign of Edward III.[5]

Daniel's failure to complete his major works is partially attributable to his own confusion and ambivalence. He may have regretted the diminished "virilitie" of his own age, when "more came to be effected by wit then by the sword," but his praise for aristocratic belligerence could not go too far. Yet while he could not oppose the "greater improuement of the Soueraigntie" of his own time, he could forestall its eventual triumph by resisting narrative closure.[6] The result is a narrative impasse in which the opposing forces remain perpetually suspended, reflecting Daniel's inability to choose between them.

It was an expedient that proved more frustrating than satisfying. Daniel's unhappiness because of his failure to finish his most ambitious work is manifest in his dedication of another piece, *Philotas*, to Prince Henry in 1605. Referring to *The Civil Wars*, he announces that "I grieue for that unfinisht frame / Which thou deare Muse didst vow to sacrifice / Vnto the bed of Peace," and he complains that it must remain unfinished without further patronage.[7] On the other hand, the difficulties *Philotas* caused him with the authorities prompt fears that he has "outliu'd the date / Of former grace, acceptance, and delight" as well as a desire that the verses inspired by Elizabeth's reign "had neuer come to light" (*Philotas*, p. 99). Daniel's torturous ambivalence persisted. Although he declares in this dedication that he "has sung enow, / And more then will be heard," having decided it is better "not to write, as not be understood" (p. 99), he went on to complete one more book of *The Civil Wars* and published a revised edition in 1609.

Daniel's difficulties with his material can also be attributed to his choice of genre, epic history. He boasted of his commitment to historical verity, announcing in the opening stanzas of *The Civil Wars*, "I versifie the troth; not Poetize" (*CW*, p. 72). This commitment to truth distinguished him, in his own eyes, from his contemporaries, most notably poets like Spenser who were caught up in the vain and fictive images of chivalric romance. He emphasized the contrast from the beginning of his career, writing in one of the *Delia* sonnets:

> Let others sing of Knights and Palladines,
> In aged accents, and vntimely words:
> Paint shadowes in imaginary lines,
> Which well the reach of their high wits records.[8]

In dedicating *The Civil Wars* to Elizabeth in 1601, he also distinguishes his own labors from those who have "vainely entertained / Thy land, with ydle shadowes to no end" (p. 65). The contrast with the "historicall fiction" of *The Faerie Queene* could not be more pointed. Daniel's difficulty arises from his subordination of poetry to his conception of historic truth. His work becomes uniquely vulnerable to the conflicts and contradictions of past and present history partly because it is, in Sidney's words, "captived to the truth of a foolish world."[9] Moreover, whereas Daniel insists that history's "acted mischiefs cannot be vnwrought" by poetry's "imagined good" (p. 312), the reverse effect occurs in his own poetry, which is "vnwrought" by its proximity to current events. Daniel's poetry finally failed to comprehend and mediate the conflicts of his period because it failed to provide him with the necessary detachment and distance.

In *The Civil Wars* Daniel's ambivalence and confusion about his subject is manifest in the split between his declared narrative scheme and its actual development. At several points near the beginning he earnestly sets forth his didactic design. In the dedication of the 1601 edition to the Queen he says that he intends to

> Bring here this worke of Warre, whereby was gain'd
> This blessed vnion which these wounds redrest,
> That sacred Concord which prepar'd the way
> Of glory for thee onely to enjoy.
>
> (*CW*, p. 65)

In the dedication of the 1609 edition to the Countess of Pembroke he says he plans

> to shewe the deformities of Ciuile Dissension, and the miserable euents of Rebellions, Conspiracies, and bloudy Reuengements, which followed (as in a circle) upon that breach of the due course of Succession, by the Vsurpation of Hen.4; and thereby to make the blessings of Peace, and the happinesse of an established Gouernment (in a direct Line) the better to appeare: I trust I shall doo a gratefull worke to my Countrie, to continue the same, unto the glorious Vnion of Hen.7: from whence is descended our present Happinesse.
>
> (p. 67)

Finally, in the opening stanzas, after lamenting the wasteful horrors of the civil wars, he poses this rhetorical question:

> Yet now what reason haue we to complaine?
> Since hereby came to the calme we did inioy;
> The blisse of thee Eliza; happie gaine
> For all our losse.

(p. 71)

The historical scheme is initially teleological, based on the orthodox Tudor mythology, in which the discords of the fifteenth century are reconciled by the triumph of Henry VII and his marriage to Elizabeth of York. From this perspective the Wars of the Roses become a *felix culpa*, whose savage conflicts lead to the blessed harmony of Tudor rule.

Nevertheless, the actual narrative unfolds along entirely different lines, fatalistic and cyclical rather than progressive.[10] History is seen as a sequence of transitory advances and inescapable declines. Peace is never a stable achievement nor an especially honorable or attractive goal; instead it is ennervating and emasculating, making Daniel's own age a "time not of that virilitie as the former" (*Works*, 4:77). In *The Civil Wars* England lurches and oscillates helplessly between the sluggish inertia of peace and the chaotic horrors of war. The belief in the inevitability of decay is deeply ingrained in Daniel's writings, and it is asserted early in *The Civil Wars* when he declares that he will show "How things, at full, do soone wex out of frame" (*CW*, p. 72).[11] This viciously circular pattern is repeated throughout *The Civil Wars*, and it is literally endless.

Daniel's fatalism wreaks havoc with his nominal moral design. *The Civil Wars* is supposed to be a simple tale of crime and punishment and redemption, but redemption is indefinitely deferred, and crime and punishment "as in a circle" are endlessly repeated. Indeed, the issue of guilt is muddled from the beginning by confusion about the origins and consequences of the crime. The opening stanzas of the poem reveal that the succession was breached long before Bullingbrook's supposedly original sin, with no dire results. The Norman conquest made "the succession doubtful, [and] rent / This new-got State, and left it turbulent" (*CW*, p. 73). This turbulence continues through the reigns of ten kings, stirring up

> The violence, of Princes, with debate
> For titles, and the often mutinies
> Of Nobles, for their ancient liberties
> (p. 73)

No great harm has resulted from these struggles. On the contrary, under Edward III England has "her greatest height attain'd / Of powre, dominion, glorie, wealth, and State" (p. 73).

The role of Edward III, the ruler immediately preceding Richard II, in the ensuing tragedy is also muddled. In *The Collection of the History of England* Daniel treats the murder of Edward II as a disruption of the succession, and though he exempts the prince from any blame, Edward III's offspring must still suffer for this wicked deed:

> The iudgement of God fell heauily, not onely vpon the great contriuers, but even vpon the whole Kingdome: and what the issue of this present Prince, whose throne (though without his guilt) was thus set vp on his fathers bloud, sustained in after times, the many imbrued Scaffolds, the diuerse bloudy fields, the infinite slaughters in the ciuill discord of their diuided families, which the consumed race of the most part of all this present Nobility will testifie.
>
> (*Works*, 5:208)

In *The Civil Wars* there is no reference to a bloodstained throne or the judgment of God. Edward III's succession is described, with punning irony, as a triumphant success:

> But now, this great Succeeder, all repaires
> And reinduc't that discontinued good:
> He builds vp strength & greatnes, for his heires,
> Out of the virtues that adornd his blood:
> He makes his Subiects Lords of more then theirs;
> And sets their bounds farre wider then they stood.
> His powre, and fortune, had sufficient wrought,
> Could but the State haue kept what he had got.
> (*CW*, p. 76)

Under Edward's successor, Richard II, England suffers a terrible reversal, but it is not presented as divine retribution for the disruption of the succession. Because Edward's heir, the Black Prince, dies before he does, his grandson succeeds him as King, and the troubles that lead to civil war begin during the latter's protectorate:

> But now the Scepter, in this glorious State,
> Supported with strong powre and victorie,
> Was left vnto a Child, ordain'd by fate
> To stay the course of what might growe too hie:
> Here was a stop, that Greatnesse did abate,
> When powre vpon so weake a base did lie.
> For, least great fortune should presume too farre,
> Such oppositions interposed are.
>
> (*CW*, p. 76)

Edward's majestic achievements come to grief because the ordinances of fate automatically check "the course of what might growe too hie." The forces at work here are growth and decay rather than sin and punishment, and the operations controlling them are more mechanical than providential.

When Daniel turns to the central conflict of *The Civil Wars*, his fatalism blurs the opposition between Richard II and Bullingbrook, undercutting the legitimacy of both sides. Certainly the latter's rebellion against legitimate authority is frequently rebuked. When Bullingbrook blames the King for provoking him by tyrannous abuse and presents himself as the champion of liberty and justice, a figure called the Genius of England dismisses these claims as the self-serving arguments of an ambitious mind. Similarly, the sympathy of the "multitude" for Bullingbrook's cause, which stems from their own afflictions, is derided as the fickle murmuring of "the malcontented sort" who seek change for its own sake (*CW*, pp. 88–89). At the same time, Daniel takes a surprisingly jaundiced view of the reaction of the "grauer sort" who are prepared to endure the wrongs that princes do for the sake of social order: "Since wise men euer haue preferred farre / Th'vniustest peace, before the iustest warre" (p. 89). Their quietism is rejected as an empty and self-serving rationalization:

> Thus they considered, that in quiet sate,
> Rich or content, or else vnfit to striue:
> Peace-louer wealth, hating a troublous State,

> Doth willing reasons for their rest contriue:
> But, if that all were thus considerate,
> How should in Court, the great, the fauour'd thriue?
> Factions must be, and these varieties:
> And some must fall, that other-some may rise.
>
> (p. 90)

Despite his professed allegiance to "the blessings of Peace," Daniel equates it here with sluggish inertia and complacency, contrasting it with the vigorous energies of factional opposition and "purging Warre" (p. 91). Yet Daniel's attitude toward both war and peace remains profoundly ambivalent: his equivocations are elaborated with no clear moral resolution in a series of paradoxes later in the work:

> O warre! begot in pride and luxurie,
> The child of malice, and reuengeful hate;
> Thou impious good, and good impietie,
> Thou art the foul refiner of a State;
> Vniust-iust scourge of mens iniquitie,
> Sharpe-easer of corruptions desperate.
> Is there no means, but that a sin-sicke Land
> Must be let bloud with such a boysterous hand?
>
> (p. 165)

Daniel sees history as a sequence of mechanical fluctuations between peace and war, and he clearly cannot decide which he prefers.

The Civil Wars offers occasional respites from this vicious circle of constant discord, moments when history promises to take another, healthier direction. The "actiue Raigne" of Henry V presents a far more heroic story of foreign conquests, one that constitutes an alternative to the poem's base plot of recurrent catastrophe. As in Shakespeare, Daniel's King succeeds in channeling his subjects' aggressions into foreign campaigns:

> He brings abrode distracted Discontent,
> Disperst ill humors into actions hie;
> And to vnite them all in one consent,
> Plac't the faire marke of glorie in their eye.
>
> (*CW*, p. 182)

At home a true *discordia concors* is achieved since Henry "cherished the ofspring of his foes; / And his Competitors to grace did bring" (pp. 186–187). Unfortunately, Henry's reign is only a brief interlude, "so happy a meane-while," in the inexorable cycle of decay (p. 186). Civil war persists because "the irritated blood, / Enduring not it selfe, it selfe assail'd" (p. 187). The organic forces of decay prove stronger than Henry's heroic triumphs.

The dead monarch himself appears to ask "great ELIZA" to commission a record of his deeds and to rebuke the poets of Daniel's "Vngrateful times" for neglecting them, in words that echo Daniel's own:

> Why do you seeke for fained Palladines
> (Out of the smoke of idle vanitie)
> Who may giue glory to the true designes,
> Of Bourchier, Talbot, Neuile, Willoughby?
> Why should not you striue to fill vp your lines,
> With wonders of your owne, with veritie?
> T'inflame their ofspring with the loue of good,
> And glorious true examples of their Blood.
>   What euerlasting matter here is found,
> Whence new immortall Illiads might proceed!
> That those, whose happie graces do abound
> In blessed accents, here may haue to feed
> Good thoughts, on no imaginarie ground
> Of hungry shadowed, which no profite breed;
> Whence musicke-like, instant delight may growe;
> Yet, when men all do knowe, they nothing knowe.
>   (*CW*, p. 179)

This is clearly intended as a reproach to authors of chivalric romance, such as Spenser; but the King's next reproof is squarely aimed at Daniel himself:

> And why dost thou, in lamentable verse,
> Nothing but blood-shed, treasons, sinne and shame,
> The worst of times, th'extreame of ills, rehearse?
>   (p. 179)

Daniel's excuse is generic decorum. He is bound to the "sadder Subiect" of civil war rather than the heroic victories of foreign combat, a task he must complete before he undertakes "immortall Illiads." He never completes that task.

Yet Daniel resolves to finish in a section of Book VI added to the 1601 edition. He also attempts a kind of mythopoetic overview of the ceaseless discord of his narrative, allowing another temporary break from its otherwise inescapable antagonisms. He introduces the figure of Nemesis, who instructs Pandora to unleash havoc on the previously peaceful states of Europe. Her implements will be those two pernicious inventions of the late Middle Ages, the printing press and gunpowder:

> two fatall Instruments,
> The one to publish, th'other to defend
> Impious Contention, and proud Discontents.
> (*CW*, p. 216)

Daniel then declares that Queen Elizabeth alone shall be exempt from the dire workings of Nemesis, and "no distresse shall touch her Diadem" (p. 218). Prophecies of a Tudor truce are reaffirmed, a time when "the conioyned aduerse powers" are united in "blessed vnion" and produce a "sacred branch" descending to Daniel's own day (p. 218). The Tudor myth is once again invoked, but it remains shadowy and remote, a goal never attained by the narrative of the poem.

By looking backward to the Middle Ages rather than forward to his own times, Daniel provides a far more alluring escape from the poem's hostilities. According to his marginal note, medieval Christendom was "at this time in the hands of seuerall Princes, and Commonwealths, which quietly gouerned the same: for, being so many, and none ouer-great, they were lesse attemptiue to disturbe others, & more carefull to keepe their owne, with a mutuall correspondence of amitie" (*CW*, p. 214). These countries and their subjects lived

> At-one with their desires, friends with Debate,
> In peace with Pride, content with their owne gaine,
> Their bounds containe their minds, their minds appli'd
> To haue their bounds with plentie beautifi'd.
> (p. 215)

Here is a profoundly attractive, if highly implausible, vision of innocence and vibrant harmony: debate flourishes between friends, and pride coexists with peace.

A romantic primitivism colors Daniel's view of the Middle Ages, but there is more than mere nostalgia behind it. The same political yearnings that prompted the Elizabethan chivalric revival and the antiquarians' interest in feudalism are also at work here: the desire for a model of peaceful coexistence between sovereign authority and the privileged subject. For Daniel, it seems, the Middle Ages provided a more appealing model than his own age.[12] Arthur Ferguson finds this odd, but he notes the most salient feature of Daniel's medievalism: "Curiously enough, Daniel admired the medieval unity of faith, yet felt that the civil virtues of the age stemmed from a de-centralized polity."[13] The absence of any central autocratic authority is essential, in Daniel's view, to the tranquil amity of the period.

Daniel's version of medieval Europe in *The Civil Wars* resembles his account of early Britain in *The Collection of the History of England*. In the later work his political primitivism and preference for the diffusion of authority are clearer. Before "the Romans made it a tributary Prouince to their Empire," Britain enjoyed an Edenic innocence and natural freedom protected by its remote insularity: as long as "it lay secluded out of the way, so it seemed out of the knowledge of the world" (*Works*, 4:86). The country was "deuided into a multitude of petty regiments, without any entire rule or combination," and there were no kings, only commanders of these regiments who ruled "without any... great iurisdiction, within those small limits they held" (4:87–88). Their lack of central authority makes them as vulnerable as the territories discovered in the New World "and generally all other countries are in their first, and naturall free nakednesse, before they come to bee taken in; either by some predominant power from abroad, or grow to head within themselves, of strength, and vnderstanding to ouer-maister, and dispose of all about them; introducing such formes of rule, as ambition, or other necessities shall beget" (4:87). Unable to resist "the power of a well-vnited State," Britain fell to the Roman empire and lost "the peace, and liberty" the country had enjoyed in its innocence (4:88). After its defeat the form of rule introduced was monarchy, and the British "made it now their custome to haue Kings, the instruments of servitude" (4:90–91).

Daniel's conception of kings as "instruments of servitude" betrays his fundamental and unresolved ambivalence toward royal authority. He insists throughout his work on his "zeale / To Kings and unto right, to quietnesse" (*Philotas*, p. 99). Nevertheless, he covertly repines at the "greater improuement of the Soueraigntie" in his own time, and instead of bringing his histories up to the present, as he promised, he keeps extending them further backward, seeking a lost innocence and liberty in his country's remote past. A utopian ideal of *discordia concors* flourishes amidst the feudal states of medieval Christendom and the "petty regiments" of ancient Britain, but it cannot withstand the encroachment of "some predominant power" from without or within.

Daniel's regard for this chivalric ideal is a major source of his fascination with England's civil wars. He can scarcely justify rebellion against "Kings, the instruments of servitude," but occasionally he takes a more positive view of opposition to them. Indeed, despite his conventional horror at the crimes and sorrows of civil war, Daniel sometimes regards it as another, especially strenuous form of *discordia concors*—brutal but invigorating. Looking back on it from the perspective of his own "neglected times," he clearly admires the nearly equal contest between the King and his overmighty subjects of an earlier age:

> For, heere, we looke vpon another Crown,
> An other image of Nobilitie
> (Which ciuile Discord had not yet brought down
> Vnto a lower range of dignity);
> Vpon a Powre as yet not ouer-flowne
> With th'Ocean of all-drowning Sov'raintie.
> These Lords, who thus against their Kings draw swords,
> Taught Kings to come, how to be more then Lords.
>
> (*CW*, p. 240)

The lords' opposition eventually proves their undoing because it only teaches kings how to defeat and dominate them, although for a time it preserves their ancient liberties and dignity.

Here and elsewhere Daniel seems to be drawn to civil war as the last and only means of maintaining the rights of knighthood against the encroachments of "all-drowning Sov'raintie," and this explains his attraction to the subject. The influence of his source, Lucan's *Civil War*—or, as it was commonly known, the *Pharsalia*—is clearly discernible in this regard. This unfinished epic of first-century Rome was a popular school text of the sixteenth century and was highly regarded by many Elizabethan writers. Barnaby Googe and George Turberville both attempted translations of the work, and Christopher Marlowe's translation of Book I was published in 1600.[14] Yet despite its importance as an Elizabethan classic, the *Pharsalia* was a profoundly subversive poem in its fierce republican sympathies and hatred of tyranny. Lucan's radical sentiments are masked by his censure of civil discord and his flattery of the reigning emperor, but these are apparently deliberately duplicitous.[15] Although the wellborn youth was initially favored by Nero, his rise through the senatorial ranks and his political independence eventually provoked the Emperor to ban the poet's work. Lucan then took a leading role in a conspiracy to assassinate Nero, but the plot was discovered, and he was arrested and forced to commit suicide before the *Pharsalia* was completed. Lucan's epic depicts Caesar from the start as a clever but villainous tyrant, whose murder is gleefully anticipated as the epic's fitting conclusion and a precedent, or exemplum, perhaps to justify Nero's assassination.[16] Both plots were cut short by Lucan's arrest and death.

Lucan too is horrified by civil war, and he regards the battle at Pharsalus, where Caesar defeated Pompey, as a catastrophe which altered Rome's destiny and "undid the work of the past." Nevertheless, he also sees civil war as the only way of opposing tyranny; according to a prophecy made in Book I of the *Pharsalia*, the country's freedom depends on its perpetuation: "This frenzy will last for many years; and it is useless to pray Heaven that it may end: when peace comes, a tyrant will come with it. Let Rome prolong the unbroken series of suffering and draw out her agony for ages: only while civil war lasts shall she henceforth be free."[17] Daniel hardly subscribes to

Lucan's republican politics, but he was deeply influenced by the *Pharsalia's* agonistic view of history. Moreover, his attitude toward civil discord shifts from moralistic condemnation, to neutral resignation to its inevitability, and then, at points, to an affirmation of its invigorating energies. In Daniel, as in Lucan, the civil wars never end, and their indefinite continuation forestalls the dead stasis of an ennervating peace.

Daniel cannot openly declare, even to himself, his desire for continuing civil war, but his imagery in the previous passage and another just before it, describing the swelling hopes of the rebellious Duke of York, indicates his resistance to the triumph of "all-drowning Sov'raintie." The equation of the monarchy with the ocean, and the nobility with the rivers, is a figure Daniel uses frequently, and Laurence Michel shrewdly defines the political conflict behind it: "The image of a river, springing obscurely but strengthened with tributaries until it becomes mighty and powerful, destined to lose its sovereignty in the ocean but sometimes giving battle before submitting, is a favorite one of Daniel's in describing the rise of rebellious factions. But the use of the image is also indicative of Daniel's never resolved dichotomy of feeling about the sacredness of kingship on the one hand and the magnanimity of some of the engulfed nobles on the other."[18] The figure conflates the idea of feudal tribute with the image of a tributary river, wishfully implying that tribute might be withheld, at least for a time. As Bullingbrook rides in triumph into London, he is compared to the Thames, exultantly swollen with its own power:

> And looke, howe Thames, inricht with many a Flood,
> And goodly Riuers (that haue made their Graues,
> And buried both their names and all their good
> Within his greatnes, to augment his waues)
> Glides on with pompe of Waters, vnwithstood,
> Vnto the Ocean (which his tribute craues)
> And layes vp all his wealth, within that powre,
> Which in it selfe all greatness doth deuowre.
>
> (*CW*, p. 102)

The ambiguity of the last couplet underscores the vainglorious futility of such resistance. In Lucan's *Pharsalia* Caesar crushes a mutiny and enters Rome to become both consul and dictator, and he scornfully makes the same point by boasting of his easy victory over his opponents: '"Tis as if all the rivers threatened to withdraw the waters they mingle with the sea."[19] Yet this was the pride that preceded Caesar's fall, for Lucan intended to conclude the *Pharsalia* with a triumphant act of tyrannicide, a conclusion thwarted by his own death. Daniel would never have even contemplated such desperate measures in his art or life. Nevertheless, his narrative still blocks the historic triumph of "all-drowning Sov'raintie" by ending before the event and indefinitely prolonging the civil wars.

As I have suggested earlier, Daniel was not satisfied with this narrative irresolution. Although he ends the last book of the 1601 edition by confessing that his muse, "Weary with these embroylements, faine would stay / Her farther course, unwilling to proceed" (*CW*, p. 265), he still hoped to complete *The Civil Wars* for several years afterward. In *A Panegyrike Congratvlatorie*, addressed to James I in 1603, Daniel subsequently urged his muse to press on and finish the work "That long hath laine vndone," so that he can finally "bring sterne discord to agree, / And bloudy warre into a quiet bed" (*Works*, 1:160). Two years later, in his dedication of *Philotas* to Prince Henry, he still remained torn between writing nothing more and pressing on to completion. He managed to write one more book for the 1609 edition, which he dedicated to one of his earliest patrons, the Countess of Pembroke, but the narrative progress of the work is limited, extending only as far as Edward IV's defeat of Henry VI at Towton, "our great Pharsalian Field" (*CW*, p. 266), and ending with the machinations of England's kingmaker, the Earl of Warwick.

This edition ends with an indeterminate debate between Warwick and his confessor. Thwarted in his plans for a French match by the new King's impetuous marriage to Elizabeth Grey and threatened by Edward's growing independence, the Earl has withdrawn to Warwick castle to plot yet another revolt against "th'ungratefull boy" he has placed on the throne (*CW*, p. 292). In these final scenes Warwick's confessor tries to allay the Earl's ultimately aimless "feuer of Ambition," while urging him to

> Inioy now what you wrought-for, in this sort
> (If great-mens Endes be to enioy their Endes)
> And knowe, the happiest powre, the greatest port,
> Is onely that which on it selfe depends.
> Heere haue you State inough to be a Cort
> Vnto your selfe; here, where the world attends
> On you, not you on it, obserued sole:
> You, else-where but a part, are heere the whole.
>
> (p. 289)

Rest and withdrawal are attractive prospects, but Warwick cannot embrace them because his fate compels him to act:

> I knowe, that I am fixt vnto a Sphere
> That is ordayn'd to moue. It is the place
> My fate appoints me; and the region where
> I must, what-euer happens, there, imbrace.
> Disturbance, trauaile, labor, hope and feare,
> Are of that Clime, ingendred in that place.
> And action, best, I see, becomes the Best.
> The Starres, that haue most glorie, haue no rest.
>
> (p. 291)

Moreover, there is no real alternative to this futile aggression because "peace can cut our throats as well as war"; its ruinous and emasculating effects are simply more insidious, "wasting all the Martiall store / Of heat and spirit (which graceth Manlinesse)" (p. 292).

Even in the final edition the poem's contempt for the peaceful order, which it moves toward but never attains, persists, and thus this version also ends in irresolution. It never reaches "that glorious holy-day / Of Vnion, which this discord reagreed" (*CW*, p. 265), nor does it reconcile its oppositions. The confessor's thoughts are recounted in the penultimate stanza of Book VIII, and they anticipate the religious solution embraced by later seventeenth-century poets:

> Here, would the reuerent Father haue reply'd,
> That it were far more Magnanimitie,

> T'indure, then to resist: that we are ty'd
> As well to beare the inconueniencie
> And straynes of Kings and States; as to abide
> Vntimely raynes, tempests, sterilitie,
> And other ills of Nature that befall:
> Which we, of force, must be content withall.
>
> (p. 293)

The confessor's notion of magnanimity resembles "the better fortitude / Of patience and heroic martyrdom" (IX. 31–32) affirmed by Milton in *Paradise Lost*.[20] It also parallels Thomas Traherne's synthesis of Aristotelian and Christian morality: "Magnanimity and Contentment are very near allyed,... Fortitude and Patience are Kindred too to this incomparable Vertue."[21] In Traherne's revision of the honor code the Great Soul finds its satisfaction and center in God and moves beyond the ambitions, contentions, and honors of this world. However, in *The Civil Wars* the priest is denied a chance to utter such thoughts because a messenger arrives bearing news of the arrival of the Duke of Clarence, the King's brother and a fickle ally in the Earl of Warwick's attempted coup. In the last stanza Warwick "breakes-off" their debate and proceeds "to worke vpon...these high purposes / He had conceiv'd in discontentednes" (p. 293). Counsels of peace and patience provide no satisfactory resting place, and Warwick compulsively persists in his futile and desperate exertions. The poem itself also abruptly "breakes-off," perpetually suspended between war and peace.

This same irresolution informs much of Daniel's later poetry. The verses addressed to royalty praise peace and restraint. In *A Panegyrike Congratvlatorie* he declares that England has achieved a glory greater than ever with James's accession because:

> What heretofore could neuer yet be wrought
> By all the swords of pow'r, by bloud, by fire,
> By ruine and distruction; here is brought
> To passe with peace, with loue, with ioy, desire.
>
> (*Works*, 1:144)

A verse epistle to Prince Henry, recently discovered and attributed to Daniel by John Pitcher, discourages foreign war and colonial conquest, urging the Prince to cultivate domestic industry instead:

> Iudge whether it be not the better farr
> To reape the fruitfull harvest of a peace
> Then sow the tragicq miseries of warr
> That will your trouble, not yor state increase.[22]

As Pitcher points out, this advice is repeated in *Tethys Festival*, the masque Daniel composed in 1610 to celebrate Henry's investiture as Prince of Wales, when a Triton declares the sufficiency of the united kingdom Henry will inherit. This "spacious Emperie...will be world enough to yeeld / All workes of glory [that] euer can be wrought"; Henry is urged not to "passe the circle of that field" whose insularity protects him (*Works*, 2:315).[23] *The Queenes Arcadia* also presents a "little angle of the world... / Which hath shut out of doore, all t'earth beside" (3:250) a domain as securely "out of the way" as early Britain is said to be in Daniel's *History of England*.

The verse he dedicated to his aristocratic patrons presents a different, more audaciously heroic picture, for Daniel was still enthralled with the daring and glorious exploits of Elizabeth's regime, a fixation that made him feel he had become "the remnant of another time" (*Philotas*, p. 98). Writing in 1609, he acknowledged in his dedication to Book VIII of *The Civil Wars* "those bright starres, from whence / Thou hadst thy light, are set for euermore" (*CW*, p. 266), but his loyalty and fascination persisted. When Mountjoy died in 1606, Daniel praised him in *A Funerall Poeme Vpon the Earle of Deuonshire* for conquering Ireland and thus opening a way to extend England's empire still further:

> Without which out-let, England thou hadst bin
> From all the rest of th'earth shut out, and pent
> Vnto thy selfe, and forst to keepe within,
> Inuiron'd round with others gouernment;
> Where now by this, thy large imperiall Crowne
> Stands boundlesse in the West, and hath a way

> For noble times, lest to make all thine owne
> That lyes beyond it, and force all t'obay.
>
> (*Works*, 1:178)

The dreams of imperial dominion and crusading militarism inspired by Elizabethan chivalry continued to haunt Daniel's imagination despite the new King's zeal for peace. Daniel could never finally decide which condition, war or peace, he believed best.

The work that most clearly betrays Daniel's lingering uncertainty toward the heroes and ideals of Elizabethan chivalry is his play *Philotas*. Suspicions that the play alluded to the Essex conspiracy were well founded, as Laurence Michel has shown.[24] Philotas is a powerful and popular noble at the court of Alexander the Great. His worst offenses are careless indiscretion and noble arrogance. His slighting remarks about Alexander's pretensions are revealed by his mistress to his enemies, and Alexander is irritated that Philotas attributes his awards of high office and elevation over his peers "rather [to] his desarts, / Than the effects of my grace any way" (*Philotas*, p. 115). Philotas's presumption recalls Essex's insistence on the power of his own inherent "active virtues…[to] draw on a prince to bestow a marshal's ofice." Philotas is driven by noble ambition and a sense of his own magnanimity, but he does not oppose Alexander's rule. Nevertheless, Daniel shows that "they that have power to hurt, and will do none," can provoke the fears of those above them regardless of what they do:

> But this is still the fate of those that are
> By nature of their fortunes eminent,
> Who either carried in conceit too farre,
> Do worke their owne or others discontent,
> Or els are deemed fit to be supprest,
> Not for they are, but that they may be ill.
>
> (p. 132)

Caught up in the conspiracy forming against Alexander, Philotas is initially presented as an innocent bystander, but his failure to inform his sovereign is used against him. Following an unfair trial arranged by his enemies, Philotas is subjected to torture, which he endures bravely for a time until, according to the Nuncius (a character who functions as a chorus), he cravenly collapses, admitting his own guilt and accusing all his friends as well:

> and so forgot
> Himselfe that now he was more forward to
> Confesse, than they to urge him thereunto.
> (*Philotas*, p. 156)

Essex also shocked his supporters by his sudden change from "death-defying hero" to "abject penitent," accusing everyone, including his sister, of leading him astray.[25] However, by placing his account of the protagonist's collapse in the mouth of the Nuncius, Daniel may have intended to cast doubt on the offical versions of both deaths; for Philotas has warned us in his last speech to the court that

> what I here do speake, I know, my Lords,
> I speake with mine owne mouth, but other where
> What may be sayd I say, may be the words
> Not of my breath, but fame that oft doth erre.
> (p. 146)

Nevertheless, Daniel's final attitude toward his protagonist and toward Essex is profoundly confusing. In the "Apology" that follows the play, he takes Philotas's confession of treason at face value and praises the "graue and worthy Councellors" who prosecuted Philotas so maliciously (*Philotas*, p. 156). As Joan Rees points out, such a conclusion "by no means squares exactly with the impressions which the play itself produces."[26] Daniel could be simply attempting to placate the censorious authorities; he also wrote a letter to Robert Cecil, the "prime mover of the prosecution against Essex," offering to withdraw the play "yf it shall seeme sknendulous [*sic*] to any."[27] The inconsistencies of the play may also derive from Daniel's characteristic ambivalence regarding the conflict between sovereign authority and noble ambition, an ambivalence aggravated by his personal feelings for Essex. He concludes his "Apology" by asking his readers not to draw any parallels between Philotas and "the late Earl of Essex. It can hold in no proportion but only in his weaknesses, which I would wish all that loue his memory not to reuiue" (p. 157). Even as he denies the association, he ends up reinforcing it.

Daniel's defense of himself and his play is characteristically contradictory. He declares rather disingenuously that the subject was "so farre from the time, and so remote a stranger from the climate of our present courses," that he "could not imagine that Enuy or ignorance could possibly haue made it, to take any particular acquaintance with vs, but as it hath a generall alliance to the frailty of greatnesse, and the vsuall workings of ambition, the perpetuall subjects of bookes and Tragedies" (*Philotas*, p. 156). He asserts here that the play's treatment of the frailties and ambitions of the overmighty subject are matters of mere literary convention, "the perpetuall subjects of bookes and Tragedies," and that in any case he began writing it "neere halfe a yre before the late Tragedy of ours (whereunto this is now most ignorantly resembled) vnfortunately fell out heere in England" (p. 156). By calling the Essex revolt a tragedy, Daniel revives a resemblance he seeks to deny. He further undermines his own argument by declaring, "I thought the representing of so true a History, in the ancient forme of a Tragedy, could not but haue had an unreproueable passage with the time, and the better sort of men, seeing with what idle fictions, and grosse follies, the Stage at this day abused mens recreations" (p. 156). Even as he defends himself, he cannot resist indulging in a variation of his familiar boast, "I versifie the troth; not Poetize." In Daniel's view, most poetry consists of little more than "idle fictions," which pale before the force of historical verity. His work deliberately subjects poetry to events, subordinating "the ancient forme of a Tragedy" to "so true a History" here and elsewhere. Thus, the incidents of past and present history inevitably encroach on his creations. He also fails to obtain any perspective on history's contradictions because his narrowly factual notion of truth and his subservient notion of poetry lead to works that are thoroughly muddled by the conflicts they represent.

Badly shaken by the controversy stirred up by *Philotas*, Daniel wrote a letter to Mountjoy, now the Earl of Devonshire, apologizing for reviving the painful memory of the Essex conspiracy. Protesting his innocence and loyalty to his patrons, he proclaims his earnest desire to protect his own reputation as well as theirs: "I know I shall liue inter historiam temporis as well as greater men" (*Philotas*, p. 39). His determination to assert his own integrity is firm: "I will not leaue a stayne of villanie vppon my name whatsoeuer error els might skape me vnfortunately thorow mine indiscreation, & misvnderstanding of the tyme" (p. 39). "Misvnderstanding of the tyme" is a pregnant phrase for Daniel. It may imply a merely personal lapse, like his "indiscreation," or it may be a collective bias shared by all his contemporaries. In either case, in the letter written to Devonshire, he bravely resolves to transcend it. Nevertheless in the funeral poem he dedicates to Devonshire the next year he doubts his ability to do so, and in the preface to a collected edition of his poems published in 1607 he despairs completely of any escape from the "misvnderstanding of the tyme." That despair illuminates the weakness at the heart of Daniel's poetry.

In his *Funerall Poeme Vpon the Earle of Deuonshire* Daniel asserts his enduring loyalty and gratitude to his old patron, but Mountjoy's death reminds him yet again of the fall of Essex. Daniel cannot resist trying to exonerate himself one more time by justifying his own errors of judgment as opinions widely held:

> And if mistaken by the Parralax
> And distance of my standing too farre off
> I heretofore might erre, and men might tax
> My being to free of prayses, without proofe.
> But here it is not so, and yet the choyce
> Of those I made did yeald the greatest show
> Of honour and of worth, and had the voyce
> Of present times their virtues to allow.
> And if they haue not made them good, it
> No fault of mine.
>
> (*Works*, 1:172–173)

He may have eventually realized the bad taste of excusing excessive praise for one patron in a funeral tribute to another; in any case, he dropped the passage from later editions. Nevertheless, Daniel openly confesses his own vulnerability and that of his poetry to the "misvnderstanding of the tyme." The contrast with a comparable apology by Ben Jonson is striking. The latter justifies his errors in praising "some names too much" by declaring it was done "with purpose to have made them such."[28] Jonson characteristically presumes almost absolute didactic control over his subjects; failure to live up to his praises is squarely theirs and not his. Daniel presents himself as the passive, helpless victim of contemporary consensus, who merely echoes "the voyce / Of present times."

Daniel finally subordinates everything, including his own work, to the vicissitudes of history. In the prefatory verses to *Certaine Small Workes*, a collection of his poetry, he acknowledges its dependence on changing customs:

> And since the measures of our tong we see
> Confirmd by no edict of power doth rest
> But onely vnderneath the regencie
> Of vse and fashion, which may be the best
> Is not for my poore forces to contest.
>   (*Poems*, p. 5)[29]

For Daniel, the "poore forces" of his verse and all poetry were no match for the powerful forces of history. His works were too closely engaged by the political controversies and complex celebrities of his age, and he never fully understood their essential conflicts. In Daniel's verse we hear "the voyce / Of present times" speaking with heightened urgency in all its confusing contradictions.

6

Edmund Spenser:
"Furthest from ... Present Time"

The poetry and career of Edmund Spenser are closely tied to the heroes and ideals of Elizabethan chivalry. His patrons included the three aristocrats whose exploits and ambitions helped to revive chivalric values in his time. He dedicated his first work, *The Shepheardes Calender*, to Sir Philip Sidney, while in the service of the Earl of Leicester. One of his last poems, the *Prothalamion*, praises the Earl of Essex as the "Faire branch of Honor, [and] flower of Cheualrie" (*Pro* 150), and in *A View of the Present State of Ireland* Spenser looked to Essex as the only hope for conquering Ireland.[1] His major work, *The Faerie Queene*, is the most vivid literary monument of the cult of Elizabeth, drawing on "the living springs in living pageantry" of courtly tribute to the Queen.[2] At the same time, Spenser's epic reenacts "the rites of knighthood," celebrating the chivalric glory of a militant aristocracy. As the tract on Ireland and much of the poetry indicate, he firmly endorsed the Protestant crusading zeal and aggressive foreign policy of the Elizabethan *militia*. *The Faerie Queene* constitutes what David Norbrook calls the "fullest poetic embodiment of the political ideals of Sidney and his circle," adding that "it reveals the complexities and contradictions inherent in those ideals."[3]

In confronting the contradictions at the heart of Elizabethan chivalry, Spenser's works mediate them more effectively than almost any other literary or cultural text of the period. He succeeds in sustaining the chivalric compromise where others fail for several reasons. First, he maintained a greater distance from the court and the pressures of courtly performance. His actual connection to the Sidney circle and Leicester's household was quite brief, and his long residence in Ireland literally set him apart from many of his contemporaries. A far more important distinction was his lofty sense of the poetic vocation. As Richard Helgerson has shown, Spenser became a "self-crowned laureate," one of the first Elizabethan writers to undertake a serious commitment to poetry.[4] He was not hobbled, as Samuel Daniel was, by the belief that poetry was an "idle fiction" or that his own "poor forces" were no match for the "acted mischiefes" of history. Spenser scorns those who dismiss his poetry as a vain or empty fiction, proudly declaring, "To such therefore I do not sing at all" (*FQ* IV. Pr. 3). His confidence in his own poetic authority was not absolute, as his sometimes bitter defensiveness indicates, but it was an important source of strength. Finally, fortified by these convictions, Spenser chose to write in genres such as allegory and elegy, whose relation to social realities is oblique. The contrast with a writer like Daniel makes the value of these generic choices clear.

In justifying his use of allegory in his "Letter of the Avthors to Sir Walter Ralegh," Spenser describes *The Faerie Queene* as "an historical fiction, the which the most part of men delight to read, rather for variety of matter, then for profite of the ensample. I chose the historye of king Arthure, as most fitte for the excellency of his person, being made famous by many mens former workes, and also furthest from the daunger of enuy, and suspition of present time" ("Letter to Ralegh," p. 407). In *The Civil Wars* Daniel attacks Arthurian romance through the ghost of Henry V, who complains that its fictions are alluring but barren, providing only an

> imaginarie ground
> Of hungry shadowes, which no profite breed;
> Whence musicke-like, instant delight may growe;
> Yet, when men all do knowe, they nothing knowe.
> (*CW*, p. 179)

By contrast, Sir Philip Sidney defends poetry "not affirmatively but allegorically and figuratively written" on precisely these same grounds, contending that those who turn to "History looking for truth, they go away full fraught with falsehood, so in Poesy looking but for fiction, they shall use the narration but as an imaginative ground-plot of a profitable invention."[5] The "imaginative ground-plot" of poetic fiction provides an alternative, utopian space, whose truths are more edifying than those "of a foolish world," a space Paul Alpers has recently termed the "poetic domain."[6] Here the poet acquires a greater degree of creative autonomy as well as protection from the abrupt encroachments of "present time." Here he can, in Kenneth Burke's words, "fight on his own terms, developing a strategy for imposing the proper 'time, place and conditions'" on the conflicts pressing on him.[7]

Burke's idea of the poet's pugnacity is entirely fitting for Spenser—far more apposite than many assume. Spenser could be fiercely and maliciously partisan in his treatment of the conflicts of his day, as his attitudes toward Spain and Ireland indicate. More fundamentally, he seems to have seen life as a ceaseless struggle, one that is sometimes harsh and brutal but generally positive. *The Faerie Queene* is the period's fullest realization of the militant, chivalric ideal of *discordia concors*. This affirmation of discord is one source of the work's value for its own time and for times to come; its imaginative distance from the pressures of topical controversy is another. The combination gives *The Faerie Queene* its unique perspective on the major conflicts of its age.

Spenser's independence and distinction as a poet was manifest from the beginning of his career. His friend and presumed mentor, Gabriel Harvey, teases him for those qualities in their published correspondence, remarking that "Master Colin Cloute is not euery body." Harvey regards Spenser's dedication to "Mistress Poetrie" with a mixture of admiration and mockery, and he jokingly predicts that "he peraduenture, by the meanes of hir [Mistress Poetrie's] speciall favour, and some personall priviledge, may happely liue ... and purchase great landes, and Lordeshippes, with the money, which his *Calender* and *Dreames* haue, and will affourde him." Harvey touches on a sore subject here and rubs it in by quoting Spenser's words against him, citing Cuddie's complaints about the "little good

...and much lesse gayne" that poetry has brought him. By contrast, Harvey emphasizes his own practical determination to pursue "those studies and practyzes, that carrie as they saye, meate in their mouth."[8]

Harvey directed his own poetic efforts at courtly performance, but they were not a notable success. In 1578 he composed a collection of Latin verses in honor of Elizabeth's visit to Audley End, subsequently entitled the *Gratulationes Valdinenses*. One of these proposes a marriage between the Queen and Harvey's patron, the Earl of Leicester. His publication of these verses embarrassed him when the Earl's secret marriage was disclosed the next year, and his efforts in verse secured him neither patronage nor influence.[9] He was embarrassed even more by Thomas Nashe's mockery of his obsequious and affected performance before the Queen at Audley End.[10] Such embarrassments were among the occupational hazards of courtly performance. George Gascoigne had his marriage masque suppressed at Kenilworth, and his accident-prone encounter with the Queen was mocked by Robert Langham's *Letter*. Both Harvey and Gascoigne were also engaged in oddly alienated tasks, laboriously transcribing words that were not their own. Gascoigne's *Tale of Hemetes the Hermit* recounts another entertainment devised by Sir Henry Lee that Elizabeth made a point of preferring. Similarly, Gabriel Harvey presented himself as a mouthpiece or, in his own image, a parrot (*psitacus*) who repeats the eulogies composed by other poets in praise of his patron.[11] Sidney's *Lady of May* was performed at Wanstead in 1578, and although it was entirely his own composition, his masque also proved vulnerable to another voice with greater authority. The Queen had the last word, and hers was always "the best part of the play."

Edmund Spenser began his poetic career in this same orbit in 1579. His acquaintances included Harvey, Sidney, and Edward Dyer, and their courtly entertainments at Kenilworth, Audley End, and Wanstead were the immediate precedents for his own efforts—precedents he considered, apparently tried, and finally rejected. He wrote something comparable to Harvey's *Gratulationes* called the *Stemmata Dudleiana*. In a letter to Harvey describing the work, Spenser tells him that "in my owne fancie, I never dyd better: *Veruntamen te sequor solum: numquam ver assequar* [Nevertheless, I shall follow only you, but I shall never overtake you]."[12] As its title indicates, the *Stemmata Dudleiana* must have been an exercise in mythopoetic genealogy praising the Earl and his distinguished ancestors. For a writer on the make, such a composition would have been an obvious means of winning favor and patronage. Indeed, this model of the poet-patron relationship was so powerful that John Florio imagined it actually applied to Spenser and Leicester and writes in the dedication of his *Second Fruites* in 1591 "that as Achilles by Alexander was counted happy for hauing such a rare emblazoner of his magnanimitie, as the Meonian Poete; so I account him thrice fortunate in hauing such a herauld of his vertues as Spenser."[13] Leicester could indeed be "a noble Mecenas," as Florio calls him, to heralds of his virtue, as Robert Cooke's career indicates.[14] Harvey's attempt at encomium was unsuccessful, but even the otherwise luckless Gascoigne obtained a royal commission through the Earl's assistance. Yet Spenser, for all his declared anxieties about pleasing "his excellent lordship," still declined to pursue such a course. He allowed the *Stemmata Dudleiana* and its "sundry Apostrophes therein, addressed you knowe to whome," to vanish without a trace.[15]

What Spenser did instead was to write and publish the ground-breaking *Shepheardes Calender*. It was in several ways a strange move. He dedicates the work to Sir Philip Sidney, "the president [precedent] / Of noblesse and of chevalree" ("To His Booke" 3–4), and pleads for the latter's protection, but he pays Sidney no other compliment within the poem, an omission that persisted for nearly fifteen years. In the October eclogue Piers urges Cuddie to

> sing of bloody Mars, of wars, of giusts,
> Turne thee to those, that weld the awful crowne.
> To doubted Knights, whose woundless armour rusts,
> And helmes vnbruzed wexen dayly browne.
>
> ("October" 39–42)

Cuddie refuses, complaining that his betters provide neither sufficient patronage nor inspiration, thus confirming doubts about their prowess already implied by their rusty, unused armor. He even refuses to praise Elizabeth and Leicester, "the worthy whome shee loueth best" (46). However conventional his complaints that "Mecaenas is yclad in claye" (61) and "mighty manhode brought a bedde of ease" (68), these sentiments ring harshly in a poem aimed at one regarded as the "noble Mecenas" and chivalric eminence of his day.

Cuddie's complaints in *The Shepheardes Calender* recall the even harsher attacks on the "mightie Peeres" in *The Tears of the Muses*, who

> onely striue themselues to raise
> Through pompous pride, and foolish vanitie;
> In th'eyes of people they put all their praise,
> And onely boast of Armes and Auncestrie.
> (*TM* 91–94)

"Armes and Auncestrie" are, as we have seen, principal points of honor to men like Sidney and Leicester, inspiring the former to issue an open challenge to anyone who would dare impugn his family's claims to these distinctions. Spenser's devotion to the major figures and ideals of Elizabethan chivalry was qualified by a surprising skepticism toward many of its pretensions.

Spenser's April eclogue offers praise instead of criticism, evoking the courtly encomium and pastoral atmosphere of the summer progress. There are even allusions to Kenilworth's Lady of the Lake, and the eclogue recalls that event's fusion of classical and rustic motifs while establishing a new direction in its compliments to the Queen. In its praise of Elizabeth as "the flowre of Virgins" ("Aprill" 49) it anticipates the message of *The Four Foster Children of Desire* and the Accession Day tilts of the 1580s. David Norbrook sees it as "a seminal work" for the remainder of her reign, inaugurating a cult of royal virginity that Leicester and his faction were eager to promote now that he was no longer a candidate for marriage.[16]

Yet despite its approximation of courtly encomium, the April eclogue still keeps its distance, avoiding the difficulties of directly addressing the Queen. E. K., the supposed author of

The Shepheardes Calender's extensive commentary, acknowledges the difficulties of direct address in his gloss of this eclogue: "In all this songe is not to be respected, what the worthinesse of Her Maiestie deserueth, nor what to the highnes of a prince is agreeable, but what is moste comely for the meanesse of a shepheards witte, or to conceiue, or to utter. And therefor he calleth her Elysa, as through rudenesse tripping in her name: and a shepheards daughter, it being very vnfit, that a shepheards boy brought vp in the shepefold, should know, or euer seme to haue heard of a Queenes roialty" ("Aprill," Glosse). Spenser's solution is characteristic. He avoids the risks of indecorum not by drawing closer but by drawing away, increasing the distance between himself and the Queen by fictionalizing their encounter. Rather than composing a courtly entertainment along the lines of *The Lady of May*, he writes an entirely imaginative apostrophe for an encounter that never occurs. He pulls back even further by removing Colin Clout, Spenser's persona, from the poem. That shepherd is off lamenting "his great misadventure in Love" ("Aprill," Argvment), and his "laye / Of fayre Eliza" is sung by Hobbinoll (33–34). Eliza, by contrast, is said to be "in place" (131) as all her nymphs surround her, but that "place" is no place—a pastoral utopia and completely fictive Eden imagined by the poet. Spenser's adroit poetic strategy allows him much more control than he would have in an actual encounter. By making Elizabeth "Syrinx daughter without spotte, / Which Pan the shepheards God of her begot" (50–51), he makes her both poetry and the poem itself, as several critics have shown.[17] As Louis Montrose adds, she also becomes Spenser's subject in both senses of that term.[18] He can thus subdue an authority whose words were always "the best part of the play" to the power of his own words.

In *The Faerie Queene* Spenser casts off the "Shepheards weeds" of his earlier poem and embraces chivalric heroism as his grand theme. Now he will finally

> sing of Knights and Ladies gentle deeds;
> Whose prayses hauing slept in silence long,
> Me, all to meane, the sacred Muse areeds

To blazon broad emongst her learned throng:
Fierce warres and faithfull loues shall moralize my song.
(*FQ* I. Pr. 1)

Emboldened by this epic task, he also directly addresses Elizabeth, her "Majestie divine / Great Lady of the greatest Isle"
(*FQ* I. Pr. 4), and he says at various points that his work has its
beginnings and its end in her court's glorious "rites of knighthood." In his letter to Ralegh Spenser describes how each of
the quests was assigned during the time that "the Faery
Queene kept her Annuall feaste xii dayes," which many see as
an allusion to the Accession Day festivities.[19] Moreover, the
poem's Order of the Maidenhead, with its "yearely solemn
feast" and Tournament of the Girdle, is a specifically Elizabethan version of the Order of the Garter, particularly in its
almost idolatrous devotion to female chastity.[20] Spenser
devotes Book IV of *The Faerie Queene* to Friendship, the virtue
the Order of the Garter was supposed to inculcate in its
members, and that book is largely occupied with tournaments
and other chivalric rites. *The Faerie Queene* would thus appear
firmly grounded in the customs and institutions of Elizabethan
chivalry.

Nevertheless, despite these clear links to contemporary
practices, Spenser still keeps his distance from the court and its
exigencies. He does this in *The Faerie Queene* by resorting to
the multiple meanings and complex displacements of allegory,
explaining in his letter to Ralegh that even his titular figure has
more than one significance: "In that Faery Queene I meane
glory in my generall intention, but in my particular I conceiue
the most excellent and glorious person of our soueraine the
Queene, and her kingdome in Faery land" ("Letter to Ralegh,"
p. 407). Like the "imaginative ground-plot" of the April
eclogue, "Faery land" is also a largely utopian space. There are
parallels with England, but, as Rosemond Tuve explains, it is
"an England (and a society of men) which never was on sea or
land, and never will be, since they adumbrate the *perfection* of
some private virtues Spenser wishes for England and for fal-
lible men."[21]

Spenser further blurs the connections of his story to present time and space by his narrative scheme. There is a split between *The Faerie Queene*'s implied aims and its actual development that in some ways resembles the split in *The Civil Wars*. Both works constantly anticipate the dynastic triumph of Tudor rule though they never reach that end. However, unlike Daniel, Spenser resists this ideological closure consciously and deliberately through his choice of narrative technique. The reasons behind his choice are clearly stated in the letter to Ralegh, where he contrasts his own "Methode of a Poet historical" with that "of an Historiographer":

> For an Historiographer discourseth of affayres orderly as they were donne, accounting as well the times as the actions, but a Poet thrusteth into the middest, euen where it most concerneth him, and there recoursing to the thinges forepaste, and diuining of thinges to come, maketh a pleasing Analysis of all. The beginning therefore of my history, if it were to be told by an Historiographer, should be the twelfth booke, which is the last, where I deuise that the Faery Queene kept her Annuall feste xii. dayes, uppon which xii. seuerall dayes, the occasions of the xii. seuerall aduentures hapned, which being undertaken by xii. seuerall knights, are in these xii books seuerally handled and discoursed.
>
> ("Letter to Ralegh," p. 408)

If Spenser employed the historian's method, his book would begin and end at the court of Gloriana, its quests firmly guided and contained by this teleological frame. But as a poet he moves through his epic more freely, beginning wherever he chooses and thrusting "into the middest, euen where it most concerneth him." His narrative frequently shifts directions because "many other aduentures are intermedled, but rather as Accidents, then intendments" (p. 408). These adventures release him from the "intendments" of Tudor historiography and its inevitable trend toward what Samuel Daniel calls "a greater improvement of the Soueraigntie."

Episodic adventure is of course an essential structural principle of chivalric romance, making the genre deliberately open-ended and centrifugal.[22] In suggesting that Spenser follows

Ariosto more closely than Tasso, Richard Helgerson has shrewdly noted the political implications of Spenser's narrative scheme: "*The Faerie Queene*, unlike *Jerusalem Delivered*, allows no place for the representation of a powerfully centralized and absolutist governmental order. It acknowledges and celebrates a sovereign lady. But it grants a high degree of autonomy to individual knights and their separate pursuits [and] represents power as relatively isolated and dispersed."[23] The poem's lack of an ending and the marginal importance of the Faerie Queene are the secret of its success. Readers like Elizabeth Bellamy, who criticize *The Faerie Queene* for failing to fulfill its epic goals, "the founding of Troynovant...and the naming of Elizabeth as a transcendental signified," miss the point. Brooding over "the poet's unsuccessful effort to nominate Elizabeth," Bellamy blames what she sees as a failure on the work's essential "conception as an allegory," a genre whose remoteness from literal reality ensures "the absence of Elizabeth-as-Presence."[24] Allegory certainly does keep transcendent authority at a distance even as it evokes it. It is, as Maureen Quilligan says, "a genre of the fallen world.... In a prelapsarian world at one with God, there is no 'other' for language to work back to, for there has been no fatal division."[25] Yet preserving this division is precisely Spenser's intention. He sees clearly what Daniel anxiously apprehends. Were he to utter the Queen's name and submit to her authority, his own discourse and authority would cease. Spenser's chivalric allegory is designed to keep Elizabeth at a distance, allowing him the fictional space to assert his protagonists' and his own autonomy. Far more effectively than the tournaments it depicts, it pays homage to the Queen even as it foregrounds discord and division. *The Faerie Queene* thus constitutes one of the most successful symbolic acts of Elizabethan chivalry.

The essential dualism of Spenser's allegory is clearest in Book I of *The Faerie Queene*. Spenser celebrates chivalric heroism while emphasizing what Rosemond Tuve calls the "tension between the earthly chivalry and heavenly chivalry."[26] The tension is strongest on Contemplation's mount, when Red Crosse catches sight of the New Jerusalem and yearns to go there immediately. Contemplation reminds the knight of his duty to the Faerie Queene, holding out the promise of glory, the great "guerdon" of such service (*FQ* I.x.59). He also discloses Red Crosse Knight's true identity as Saint George. As *Georgos* he is a "man of earth" (52) and his "owne nations frend / And Patron" (61). Indeed, Spenser goes out of his way to give the patron saint of England and the Order of the Garter a patriotically autochthonous identity, making him the descendant of an "ancient race / Of Saxon kings" (65), as Anthea Hume points out.[27] Nevertheless, before he can be exalted to the company of the saints, he must renounce "earthly conquest" and the "guilt of bloudy field" (60). Even as the two parts of his identity promise to merge, fusing earthly and heavenly chivalry, they are pushed further apart by Contemplation's double message.

The conclusion of Book I holds out the promise of an almost apocalyptic fusion of earthly and heavenly chivalry. Red Crosse Knight's final battle with the dragon echoes both Genesis and Revelation, placing this struggle at the beginning and end of time. As David Norbrook says, "Revelation is a generic model for Book I," and many of Spenser's earliest readers read it in this light.[28] John Dixon certainly did so, as his annotations indicate. Dixon's marginalia combine scriptural parallels with ingenious topical glosses in cipher. He identifies Red Crosse as Leicester and Arthur as the Earl of Cumberland. The betrothal of Una and Red Crosse is interpreted as the accession and coronation of Elizabeth, and Red Crosse's return to service is equated with "the time of the raingne of phil: and marye."[29] Norbrook writes that for many of Spenser's contemporaries, patriotic sentiments combined with millennial expectations to inspire yearnings for a commander "who would lead the decisive battle against Antichrist."[30] Some looked to Leicester to lead this chivalric Armageddon, while others turned to Essex. In Book I and elsewhere Spenser stirs up these expectations only to dissipate them through a conclusion that is strangely anticlimactic. In singing of this battle, he conspicuously lowers his pitch to the "second tenor" (*FQ* I.xi.7). Moreover, the narrative movement, with its return to duty and lapse from

"blisfull joy" to mourning (I.xii.41), wreaks havoc with both
the providential and political chronology of Dixon's gloss.
Book I becomes, in Kenneth Gross's terms, an almost "anti-
apocalyptic fiction," consciously avoiding transcendence and
persisting in its split between earthly and heavenly chivalry.[31]

Paradoxically, the persistence of division is strongest in
Book IV, the book of Friendship. The book's nominal heroes
are Triamond and Cambell, who begin as fierce antagonists
and become loyal comrades-in-arms. Their conversion from
enmity to amity is emblematically represented by the porch of
Concord, the entryway to the temple of Venus. There Concord is personified as an "amiable Dame" flanked by Love and
Hate, two young warriors "Both strongly arm'd, as fearing one
another" (*FQ* IV.x.32). Stronger than both, she reconciles and
tempers these warring passions by forcing them to join hands.
She thus becomes the "Mother of blessed Peace, and Friendship trew" (34) as well as the most exalted embodiment of the
ideal of *discordia concors*. If this is an idealized portrait of the
Queen serenely prevailing over the fierce rivalries at court, it is
qualified by the events of the rest of the book. The Order of
the Maidenhead and the Tournament of the Girdle also closely
resemble the chivalric institutions of the Elizabethan court, but
their proceedings are far more disorderly than harmonious. If
Concord prevails in Book IV at the moment of emblematic
stasis, discord and disruption prevail in the narrative.

The girdle, which is the sign of Spenser's Order of the
Maidenhead, belongs to the absent and much-loved Florimell.
This symbol of her maiden purity and token of her favor initially divides her admirers, but Satyrane uses it for a time to
bind them together. When he first acquires it, his fellow
knights "that loved her like deare, / Thereat did greatly
grudge," so he proclaims a "solemne feast with publike turney-
ing" in order to "stop vile envy's sting" (*FQ* IV.ii.26). The
girdle will be the prize awarded to the fairest lady, and the
strongest knight "Shall to that fairest ladie be prefard" (27). In
the meantime, the elusive Florimell is declared the "ward" of all
her admirers, and "that ornament of hers pertains" as well to all

the Knights of Maidenhead (27). All are briefly united against a common foe:

> Tho each to other did his faith engage,
> Like faithfull friends thenceforth to ioyne in one
> With all their force, and battell strong to wage
> Gainst all those knights, as their professed fone,
> That chaleng'd ought in Florimell, saue they alone.
>
> (*FQ* IV.ii.28)

Florimell is beloved by all, and the collective devotion of her knights overcomes all rivalries. None makes exclusive claims on her affection, and all resist any outside challenge to their devotion. The lady's chastity is an article of faith and point of honor for all her devotees. These were the principal tenets of the cult of Elizabeth, ritually enacted in *The Four Foster Children of Desire* and every succeeding Accession Day tilt. The Elizabethan "rites of knighthood" also supposedly sustained the "goodly fellowship" of the contestants as well as loyalty to the Queen.

Nevertheless, in Spenser's account the actual tournament falls short of these aims, failing to achieve anything like chivalric friendship. Indeed, the Knights of Maidenhead find "discord harder ... to end than to begin" (*FQ* IV.i.20). On the first day of the contest the victory goes to Satyrane, the sponsor of the tournament, and Triamond and Cambell, the heroes of Book IV, share the glories of the second day, "each labouring t'aduance the others gest" (IV.iv.32). These amicable sports are disrupted on the third and final day by the arrival of a "straunger knight" in "saluage weed" (39), who proceeds to defeat all challengers and thus threaten the knights of Maidenhead with disgrace:

> Thus was Sir Satyrane with all his band
> By his sole manhood and atchieuement stout
> Dismayd, that none of them in field durst stand.
>
> (43)

The Savage Knight is Artegall in disguise, and he in turn is defeated by his lover, Britomart, who knocks him off his horse,

"Whence litle lust he had to rise againe" (44). Spenser's double entendre emphasizes the sexual comedy of this battle between savage virility and invincible chastity, and Britomart's victory over her future husband broadens the irony of this episode. A chaste woman can better defend her own honor than any of the Knights of Maidenhead since her inward virtue triumphs over their shows of strength. She magnanimously restores the "prize, to knights of Maydenhead / Which else was like to haue bene lost," but the honor regained is an empty one since she takes the "prayse of prowesse from them all away" (48). This unstable resolution is further undercut by the distribution of the prizes. Dazzling nearly all the beholders with her specious charms, the false Florimell wins the prize for beauty and chooses the cowardly Braggadochio as her champion (IV.v.22).

The Tournament of the Girdle settles nothing, and its outcome only provokes "new discord." Hostilities erupt again in canto ix when a small band of knights quarreling with one another turn against Britomart and Scudamour because they resent the defeat "which that Britonesse had to them donne, / In that late Turney for the snowy maide" (*FQ* IV.ix.28). Prince Arthur comes to the rescue "with gentle words perswading them to friendly peace," but the fractious knights turn on him, and Britomart and Scudamour must then persuade Arthur to "asswage his wrath" (35). Finally, an accord is achieved amongst "this gentle crew" (40), but although Arthur accuses Britomart's assailants of being "much to blame / To rip vp wrong, that battell once hath tried" (37), the fraudulent results of the first tournament still make a retrial necessary.

A second set of "solemne feasts and giusts" is therefore arranged in honor of the wedding of Marinell and the true Florimell. One of the few real marriages in *The Faerie Queene*, the event holds out the promise of "Some blissfull houres at last" (*FQ* V.iii.1). Indeed, the poem's recurrent narrative movement of turn and return is here, for once, benign, and Spenser's pun gives the movement an explicitly chivalric significance:

> So comes it now to Florimell by tourne,
> After long sorrowes suffered whyleare,

> In which captu'd she many moneths did mourne,
> To tast of ioy, and to wont pleasures to retourne.
>
> (1)

Aggrieved by the results of one tournament or tourney, his characters resort to a "retourne" and chivalric retrial for satisfaction. The "retourne" resembles the Tournament of the Girdle in several ways, and initially it threatens to repeat the mistakes of the first tournament. The first two days are playfully inconsequential, with "litle lost or wonne" (6). On the final day Artegall rescues Marinell while using Braggadochio's shield. When the day's combat ends, the "honour of the prize" is once again mistakenly awarded to Braggadochio, but this time Artegall intervenes, demanding "proofe" of Braggadochio's martial exertions:

> Or shew the wounds, which vnto thee befell;
> Or shew the sweat, with which thou didest sway
> So sharpe a battell, that so many did dismay.
>
> (21)

After Braggadochio cowers before him and the false Florimell simply melts away, the Knight of Justice returns the girdle to the true Florimell and a stolen horse to Guyon. Still furious with the cowardly Braggadochio, Artegall is ready to kill him, but Guyon proposes a more tempered and fittingly chivalric punishment of ritual degradation: "It's punishment enough, that all his shame doe see" (36).

Michael Leslie regards the ceremonial disgrace of Braggadochio as the climactic "resolution of the theme of chivalry in *The Faerie Queene.*"[32] The abortive results of the Tournament of the Girdle cast doubt on "the rites of knighthood" blotting "good deserts with blame" (*FQ* V.iii.38). In Leslie's analysis of chivalric themes in Spenser's verse, the "pollution of the symbols of knighthood involves the pollution, through them, of the ideal itself. The return of these chivalric symbols at the spousals tournament represents the reversal of the corruption resulting from the usurpation of Braggadochio and thus may signal the regeneration of knighthood within the poem." Leslie also sees Artegall's rebuke to Burbon for casting aside his shield as an allusion to Spenser's hopes for a renewal of the Order of the Garter "to be revealed in triumph at the end of the poem."[33] Leslie concedes that such a reform is never realized because the poem never reaches its announced end; but even if it did, his hopes for a definitive regeneration of knighthood within *The Faerie Queene* are finally too optimistic. Justice is done at the spousals tournament, and Artegall joins with Arthur to defeat the Souldan, whose fall recalls the destruction of the Armada. Together they rescue the Lady Belge from her captors, but these triumphs are followed by defeat. Artegall fails to suppress rebellion in Ireland, and by the end of Book V the Blatant Beast runs rampant, "blott[ing] good deserts with blame." Deceit is once again triumphant. Idolized and even fetishized in the Tournament of the Girdle, the chivalric symbols of chastity and honor are briefly redeemed by an act of fierce iconoclasm at the spousals tournament, but the effects of Artegall's victories over Braggadochio and all his other opponents prove only temporary. Discord persists and intensifies in Book V.

Leslie's interpretation of chivalric symbolism in *The Faerie Queene* is based on a common misunderstanding of Spenserian allegory. He contends that in Renaissance art "symbols possess a validity and an authority independent of the particular writer or artist employing them: their meaning is inherent and the artist, whether visual or verbal, discovers and uses, but does not create it."[34] Many earlier critics worked on similar assumptions, subordinating Spenser's allegory to the signs systems of Christian humanism or neoplatonism, whereas more recent critics subject the work to the beliefs of Tudor political thought. Stephen Greenblatt argues that *The Faerie Queene* always refers the "reader out to a fixed authority beyond the poem," which is, in his reading, the ruthless power of Elizabethan imperialism.[35]

Spenser was deeply bound throughout his career by the constraints of patronage and courtly politics as well as the brute exigencies of colonial power. Christian belief and chivalric ideals were no less influential. However, none of these firmly held convictions defines *The Faerie Queene* in its entirety, nor does Spenser's allegory merely affirm the ideological supremacy of one code or another. Angus Fletcher's conception of allegory is much closer to the mark, especially with regard to Spenser: "Allegories are far less often the dull systems that they are reputed to be than they are symbolic power struggles." Moreover, as Fletcher points out, these power struggles "tend to stress the equality of the two opposing forces," a factor that contributes to the irresolution of allegorical conflict.[36] Kenneth Gross calls this struggle the "allegorical agon," one that turns on itself by trying to free the mind of illusions and idols even as it generates its own.[37] In Gross's account Spenserean allegory oscillates indefinitely between iconoclasm and idolatry, each canceling out the other. Spenser's treatment of Elizabethan chivalry is typically more ambiguous than celebratory.

Spenser's detached perspective on the chivalric code is perhaps clearest in his truncated account of the spousals tournament. Some twentieth-century readers see a close correspondence to contemporary tilts in the description of the challenges and the allegorical names and devices of the contestants.[38] Spenser's cryptic account of their "deedes of armes" resembles George Peele's in its formulaic evasions: "Yet whether side was victor, note be ghest" (*FQ* V.iii.6–7). Spenser, however, dismissively cuts short his recital of these "deuicefull sights ... The pride of Ladies and the worth of Knights" (3), abbreviating what Peele or Sidney would have amplified. He declares such descriptions "worke fit for an Herauld, not for me" (3). In this passage the poet explicitly rejects the role of a "Herauld" of noble virtue, a role assigned him by John Florio in 1591. It is a quiet but striking declaration of poetic independence, in which the writer asserts his freedom from the details of courtly pomp and pageantry and the demands of merely documentary accuracy. Spenser's "treatise" will focus on more important issues, and only those truths that help "True vertue to aduance, shall here recounted bee" (3). The same distinction is forcefully made by another "self-crowned laureate," Ben Jonson, who writes in an epigram addressed "To All, to Whom I Write":

> May none, whose scatter'd names honor my booke,
>   For strict degrees of ranke, or title looke:
> 'Tis 'gainst the manners of an Epigram:
>   And, I a Poet here, no Herald am.[39]

Both writers claim a higher authority for the poet whose concern is "true virtue" rather than degrees in the social hierarchy.

In Book VI Spenser is thought to succumb to a thorough disillusionment with Elizabethan chivalry, but the feelings of defeat and division that haunt the conclusion derive from a dualism manifest from the beginning of *The Faerie Queene* as well as the last book's acknowledgment of the incompatible aims of the chivalric quest.[40] Spenser certainly does treat the trappings of Elizabethan chivalry, its armor and feigned shows, with less respect, as knightly valor, like true courtesy, becomes more inward and covert. Many knights happily cast off their armor without suffering the dire consequences previously inflicted on those who disarm. The opprobrium and injury that befall Red Crosse Knight, Burbon, and, more comically, Britomart are largely avoided in Book VI. Aldus and Calepine are more vulnerable to attack when unarmed, but Tristram is not, and the latter proudly defies the "law of armes" by defeating his armored attacker (*FQ* VI.ii.7). Calepine happily does without "his heavy arms," the better to save a baby from a bear:

> Now wanting them he felt himselfe so light,
> That like an Hauke, which feeling herselfe freed
> From bels and iesses, which did let her flight,
> Him seem'd his feet did fly, and in their speed delight.
>   (VI.iv.19)

The feeling of exultation and release in this passage is palpable, as William Nestrick says.[41] The Savage Man casually dons this same suit of armor and takes it off two stanzas later "withouten doubt or dreed" (VI.v.10). The armor's connection to its owner as well as any intrinsic symbolic value are drastically diminished by such treatment, as it becomes "warlike" (8) one moment and "cumbrous" (10) the next.

Most astonishing of all is Arthur's carelessness with his armor in the middle of the book, a lapse that places him in danger without causing him any harm:

> Wearie of trauell in his former fight,
> He there in shade himselfe had layd to rest
> Hauing his armes and warlike things vndight,
> Fearlesse of foes that mote his peace molest.
> (*FQ* VI.vii.19)

He is of course immediately discovered by one of those foes, the treacherous Turpine, but the villain is too cowardly to murder the sleeping prince by himself and turns to another for help. The other knight refuses to stoop "to such villenie" (23), and the Savage Man arrives in time to awaken Arthur, who then punishes Turpine by hanging him by the heels.

For one figure in Book VI, the gesture of disarming is deliberate and definitive. The Hermit had been a "doughty knight" (*FQ* VI.vi.4), who was

> Renowmed much in armes and derring doe:
> But being aged now and weary to
> Of warres delight, and worlds contentious toyle,
> The name of knighthood he did disauow.
> (VI.v.37)

The hermit is a traditional figure in medieval chivalric romance, appearing in Ramon Lull's *Book of the Ordre of Chyvalry* as a retired knight and expert counselor who instructs a young squire in the rules of knighthood. In the tilts and spectacles of Elizabethan chivalry Sir Henry Lee appeared frequently in the guise of a hermit. A hermit welcomed the Fairy Queen during Lee's show at Woodstock in 1575, and, in an undated entertainment, a hermit and a knight withdrew to the country to reflect on "the mutability of things" until the knight returned to joust in an Accession Day tilt. At his retirement tilt on Accession day in 1590 Lee presented himself as a hermit devoted to the Queen, a saint enshrined within a temple of vestal virgins, and in 1592 at Ditchley, his home in Buckinghamshire, he was again a hermit, who fondly recalls his youthful jousts at "the yearly tribute of his dearest love."[42] Frances Yates has carefully examined the chivalric pastoralism, "the philosophy of mutability," and the allegorical figures of the Fairy Queen, the hermit and the "clownishly clad" knights, and she finds in them "a connection beyond dispute" between Lee's chivalric spectacles and Spenser's *Faerie Queene*.[43]

The Hermit's appearance in *The Faerie Queene* could certainly have been an occasion for paying homage to Elizabeth in the familiar terms of chivalric tribute, but Spenser does nothing of the kind. On the contrary, his version of pastoral retirement is sharply opposed to Sir Henry Lee's. The Hermit in *The Faerie Queene* renounces the "name of knighthood" with a shocking finality, and he sets his armor aside forever as the embodiment of "this worlds incumbraunce" (*FQ* VI.v.37). Unlike Lee, he feels no affection or nostalgia for his former life, and Spenser pointedly remarks that he entertains his guests simply, and "Not with such forged showes, as fitter beene / For courting fooles, that curtesies would faine" (38). This Hermit's contempt for the world surpasses even that of Contemplation, who denigrates chivalric heroism in the long run but still praises Gloriana and Cleopolis while urging Red Crosse Knight to resume his quest. Praise for Gloriana is conspicuously absent from the Hermit's devotions and from much of the rest of Book VI. As William Nelson says, "The Legend of Courtesie, alone of the books of *The Faerie Queene*, contains no celebration of the Queen, her ancestry, or the country over which she rules."[44]

The desire to renounce the "worlds incumbraunce" and the "combrous armes" of chivalric combat pervades Book VI. Meliboe has also left the court to resume a "lowly quiet life" (*FQ* VI.ix.25) in the country, and he argues, as the Hermit does, for stoic self-sufficiency and control of one's desires: "But fittest is, that all contented rest / With that they hold: each hath his fortune in his brest" (28). Calidore, the hero of Book VI, is charmed by Meliboe's eloquence and Pastorella's beauty, and he too renounces the "worlds gay showes" and "glorie of the great" (27, 28) to seek "rest" from the "stormes of fortune and tempestuous fate" (31). The brigands' attack thwarts these wishful fantasies, showing that the pastoral life is just as vulnerable as any other to "warres, and wreckes, and wicked enmitie" (19). Calidore must "turne againe" (31) to his heroic duty to rescue Pastorella.

Spenser still displays considerable sympathy for his protagonist's rejection of courtly fame and service. Even as he chastens Calidore for being "Vnmyndfull of his vow and high beheast, / Which by the Faery Queene was on him layd" (*FQ* VI.x.1), he still maintains that the Knight should not "greatly blamed be" for rejecting the court's "painted show" (3) to pursue his courtship of Pastorella:

> Another quest, another game in vew
> He hath, the guerdon of his loue to gaine:
> With whom he myndes for euer to remaine,
> And set his rest amongst the rusticke sort,
> Rather then hunt still after shadowes vaine
> Of courtly fauour.
>
> (VI.x.2)

Spenser's approval of "another quest" with other aims beyond "courtly favour" affirms the inherent dualism of the chivalric code, endorsing both loyal service and self-assertion, public duty and private impulse, and holding these incompatible ideals in precarious equilibrium. There is a powerful split at work here, but I would argue that instead of leading to what David Miller calls a "fatal disjunction," it sustains a tense but invigorating compromise.[45]

Spenser not only favors this other quest but also joins it in the person of Colin Clout, his poetic alter ego from *The Shepheardes Calender*. Like the Hermit, Colin Clout renounces the world and dwells apart on Mount Acidale, "far from all peoples troad" (*FQ* VI.x.5). Here, atop this *locus amoenus*, Venus joins the three Graces and a "hundred naked maidens lilly white / All raunged in a ring, and dauncing in delight" around his own beloved "iolly Shepheards lasse" while Colin accompanies them on his pipe (11). Calidore disrupts the moment of vision, prompting the poet to shatter his pipe because he doubts its reality. For most of the dance the knight remains hidden, "Beholding all, yet of them vnespyde" (11), but he suspects that "his eyes mote haue deluded beene" (17):

> Therefore resoluing, what it was, to know,
> Out of the wood he rose, and toward them did go.
> But soone as he appeared to their vew,
> They vanisht all away out of his sight.
>
> (17–18)

Ironically, Calidore still does not know what he saw since the disappearance of the maidens may have been caused by maidenly modesty or by the evanescence of an illusion.

Behind Calidore's blunder is a rooted ignorance of the nature of allegorical vision, a suspicion that it presents only groundless illusions. These are the same suspicions voiced by another chivalric hero, Daniel's Henry V, who complains that such visions provide only an

> imaginarie ground
> Of hungry shadowes, which no profite breed;
> Whence musicke-like, instant delight may growe;
> Yet, when men all do knowe, they nothing knowe.
>
> (*CW*, p. 179)

Calidore is more courteous and less confidently close-minded. He feels the allure of these "pleasant playes" (VI.x.19) and, apologizing for disrupting them, asks the poet to tell him what they are. Colin's response is equally courteous; for both men, Mount Acidale proves a "profitable ground-plot of invention."

Colin's reply makes clear the social importance of his vision as well as its relevance to Calidore's larger quest. The poet identifies each of the dancers, from the loftiest Olympians to his own humble beloved, explaining their significance as embodiments of courtesy and civility. These last gestures toward Calidore and toward us, his readers, are what make this scene sociable rather than solipsistic.[46] In fact, Colin's vision represents a fusion of both the romantic and the heroic quests because in addition to gaining "the guerdon of his loue," he attains the goal declared in the proem to Book VI—insight into the secret, "sacred noursery / Of virtue" previously concealed "From view of men, and wicked worlds disdaine" (*FQ* VI. Pr. 3). As Colin explains afterward, the Graces who danced for him bestow "all gracious gifts" on men

> And all the complements of curtesie:
> They teach vs, how to each degree and kynde
> We should our selues demeane, to low, to hie;
> To friends, to foes, which skill men call Ciuility.
>
> (VI.x.23)

This moment of transcendent synthesis and triumph remains extraordinarily tense because it does not deny the division and discord behind its concord. The underlying tensions are clearly manifest in the apology to "Great Gloriana, greatest Maiesty," asking her to "pardon thy shepheard" for making "one minime of thy poore handmayd" by singing the latter's praises instead of the Queen's (28). Spenser tries to placate his royal auditor even as he pushes her still further from his poem's center. *The Faerie Queene*'s climactic vision of exalted civility and courtesy thus explicitly excludes Elizabeth.

The final cantos of *The Faerie Queene* push Elizabeth even farther aside. In the "Mutability Cantos" Cynthia, the goddess, with whom the Queen identified, is assaulted by Mutability— an unsettling incident despite Mutability's eventual defeat. Moreover, these verses are dominated by the personification of change and Dame Nature rather than the Faery Queene. Some readers discern a cryptic reference to Elizabeth in the last line in the invocation of "that great Sabbaoth God" (*FQ* VII.vii.2), one that conflates the sovereign's name with God's, intimating an otherwise ineffable Eli-sabbath.[47] But the royal name is never uttered, and though the poet prays for a glimpse of that final "Saboaths sight" (2), he postpones it indefinitely in a final act of displacement and deferral. The Queen and the apocalypse are kept at a distance, delaying any ultimate political or providential resolution. In the meantime, "all that moueth, doth in change delight" (2) as *The Faerie Queene* exults in its own endless *discordia concors*.

Mutability haunts the poems Spenser dedicated to his aristocratic patrons, the great heroes of Elizabethan chivalry. Several of these are elegies honoring Sidney and Leicester in death, but even the *Prothalamion*, which praises Essex in his hour of triumph, is persistently elegiac, mournfully aware of the vicissitudes of time. The elegy, like allegory, becomes a means of maintaining poetic distance and detachment. *The Ruines of Time* is dedicated to Mary Sidney and is "speciallie intended to the renowming of that noble race, from which both you and he sprong" (*RT*, p. 471). Sir Philip Sidney is indeed exalted in this poem, but Spenser's treatment of the Earl of Leicester, among others, is strangely disparaging:

> He now is dead, and all his glorie gone,
> And all his greatnes vapoured to nought,
> That as a glass vpon the water shone,
> Which vanisht quite, so soone as it was sought.
> His name is worne alreadie out of thought,
> Ne anie Poet seekes him to reuive;
> Yet manie Poets hounourd him aliue.
>
> (*RT* 218–224)

Leicester dies forgotten and unmourned, the embodiment of the "vaine worlds glorie, and unstedfast state" (43). In Spenser's odd poetic conceit both Ambrose and Robert Dudley are identified with their heraldic devices: they become two white bears who are buried as they "lay sleeping sound" in their own cave, which "Was but earth, and with her own weightinesse / Vpon them fell, and did vnwares oppresse" (469–471). In Spenser's treatment the Dudleys' deaths become almost ridiculous if not ignominious.[48] By contrast, Sidney's spirit soars aloft after a brief struggle between heaven and earth over who "should of those ashes keeper be" (665). However, the symbols that survive the fallen hero to become celestial signs are not heraldic but poetic: the swan and the harp make the "loftie flight aboue the earth" (599). Moreover, the symbols of chivalric triumph worn by the mortally wounded knight, the "manie garlands for his victories," and the "rich spoyles, which late he did purchas" (653–654), are deemed "small ioy to him" (652). The poem concludes with Mercury, the god of eloquence, descending to bear the ark of Sidney's ashes up to heaven. Even in a poem dedicated to "the renowming of that noble race" sprung from the Dudley line Spenser still refuses to be the herald of "Armes and Auncestrie" (*TM* 94). Indeed, he almost mocks the Dudleys' heraldic devices, reserving his praise for the symbols of his own vocation, poetry.

In *Astrophel*, Spenser's tribute to Sir Philip Sidney, the power of poetry is asserted even more strenuously. Here the poet's verse acquires a power as great as, or even greater than, heroic exertion. Just as Colin Clout succeeds in Book VI in discovering the "sacred noursery" of civil virtue while Calidore's quest falters, the author of this elegy achieves a political resolution beyond the grasp of his subject. Spenser aims to correct the prevailing prejudice against poetry by insisting that "verses are not vaine" (*Ast* 68). He also subtly criticizes his subject by noting the excess that destroyed the perfect balance of Sidney's virtues: "For both in deeds and words he nourtred was, / Both wise and hardie (too hardie alas)" (71–72).[49] The criticisms only grow harsher as Spenser calls Astrophel "misweening" (101), "heedlesse" (103), "vnmyndfull" (112), and, in the end, a "lucklesse boy" (142). In Spenser's highly mythopoetic account Astrophel dies as Adonis did, gored in the thigh by a boar, and Stella, "deforme[d] like him to bee" (156), dies with him; together they are metamorphosed into a flower with a star at its center.

Clorinda, Astrophel's sister—and the poet Mary Sidney—recovers from her sorrow by composing her own elegy, and Clorinda's "dolefull lay" (*Ast* 214) moves the poem in another, less morbid direction.[50] At first she is almost as distracted by grief and despair as Stella, refusing to address the heavens, whom she blames for this catastrophe, or her helpless fellow creatures, resolving instead that "to my selfe will I my sorrow mourne, / Sith none aliue like sorrowfull remaines" (19–20). Gradually, however, her song restores her to a sense of connection and community. In his suggestive analysis of pastoral elegy Paul Alpers describes it as a means of recovering community since its traditional conventions sustain a literal "convening": "Convention is precisely a poetic practice that makes up for a loss, a separation or an absence. The idea of convention...involves not only a gathering for a song on a specific occasion, but also a usage that implicitly convenes an absent predecessor—the poet who instituted the rhetorical practices exemplified here."[51] This is precisely the process enacted by Clorinda's "dolefull lay" since the company of mourners expands as she proceeds. Her plaint is first echoed by nature and then joined by "shepheards lasses" (37), and the poem concludes with the entrance of Thestylis and other mourners, who join her in lamenting Astrophel's loss. These are the other poets who contributed to the collection that Spenser's poem heads, and Spenser graciously introduces them by saying that "euerie one in order lov'd him best" (104), an oxymoron that conveys the singular intensity of their grief and the collective nature of its expression. In *Astrophel* poetry enables the contributors to recover a communal order and preserve the memory and ideals of the dead hero—proof that "verses are not vain."

One of Spenser's last works, the *Prothalamion*, was written to honor the weddings of the Earl of Worcester's daughters at Essex house in 1596 and to praise the Earl of Essex. Its vivid scenes of ceremonial splendor and chivalric glory are firmly connected to actual figures and events. The poem celebrates the Earl's victory in Cadiz, praising Essex as "Great Englands glory and the Worlds wide wonder, / Whose dreadfull name, late through all Spaine did thunder" (*Pro* 146–147):

> Faire branch of Honor, flower of Cheualrie,
> That fillest England with thy triumphs fame
>
> . . . .
>
> That through thy prowesse and victorious armes
> Thy country may be freed from forraine harmes:
> And great Elisaes glorious name may ring
> Through al the world, fil'd with thy wide Alarmes,
> Which some braue muse may sing
> To ages following.
>
> (150–160)

In the *Prothalamion* the chivalric compromise flourishes, exalting the aggressively "dreadfull name" of Essex and "Elisaes glorious name" in concert.

Yet despite its soaring hopes and strong connections to contemporary history, the *Prothalamion* begins on a note of bitter estrangement. The speaker is afflicted by "sullein care" and "discontent of my long frutilesse stay / In Princes Court" (*Pro* 5–7). He walks along the "shore of siluer streaming Themmes" to "ease my paine" (10–11). Once away from the scenes of his affliction, he sees a group of water nymphs gathering flowers for the wedding and bestowing their bouquets upon two pure white swans, symbols of the Earl of Worcester's daughters. The poet admires their beauty and compares them to the swans that draw Venus's chariot, concluding his compliment with a pun on the brides' maiden names, Somerset:

> For sure they did not seeme
> To be begot of any earthly Seede,
> But rather Angels or of Angels breede:
> Yet were they bred of Somers-heat they say
> In sweetest Season, when each Flower and weede
> The earth did fresh aray.
>
> (65–70)

One of the nymphs sings, invoking blessings on the nuptials, and her undersong is repeated by the other nymphs and again by Echo. The river Lee "murmured low" and tried to join in:

> As he would speake, but that he lackt a tong
> Yeat did by signes his glad affection show,
> Making his streame run slow.
>
> (115–118)

In the eighth stanza the poet returns with this aquatic entourage to London, reversing, as Harry Berger says, "the gesture of escape which opened the poem" and bringing it back to the historical present.[52] Nevertheless, Spenser still has difficulty fixing his thoughts on the occasion at hand, and his reverie keeps drifting back in time to his birth in the city of London, to "my most kyndly Nurse / That to me gaue this Lifes first natiue sourse" (*Pro* 128–129), and then to his presumed descent from the Spensers of Althorpe and their "house of auncient fame" (131). Two other venerable buildings along the water's edge inspire more melancholy memories. The Temple, where "now the studious Lawyers haue their bowers," was once occupied by the Knights Templars "till they decayd through pride" (134–136). Next to it stands Essex house, "a stately place" (137) and home of the Earl of Essex, but Spenser thinks instead of its former occupant, the Earl of Leicester, "that great Lorde, which therein wont to dwell, / Whose want too well now feeles my freendles case" (139–140). The "want" of a patron brings us back to the discontent that prompted the poet's wandering at the beginning of the poem. Spenser shifts directions yet again with a firm reminder of the occasion and its demands: "But Ah here fits not well / Olde woes but ioyes to tell" (141–142).

Spenser's praise for Essex is lavish and hopeful, and he anticipates still greater victories and a renewal of chivalric virtue. But despite these triumphant expectations, the mood remains profoundly elegiac. There is a feeling that while "some braue muse may sing" of the Earl's heroism, it will not be Spenser's. As Richard Helgerson says of these lines, "It is hard to tell whether he is putting himself definitively out of contention or bidding for the job. But in the refrain, with its insistence that the day is short and that his song will continue only while the Thames runs softly, we hear the sound of an ending, an impending withdrawal from the public world that this poem still celebrates."[53]

This valedictory tone and sense of an immediate ending are very strong in the final stanza. There the Earl is shown descending from the "high towers" of Essex house and proceeding to the water's edge to receive the bridal party: "Like Radiant Hesper when his golden hayre / In th'Ocean billowes he hath Bathed fayre" (*Pro* 164–165). Spenser's comparison of the Earl to the evening star evokes associations with Venus, under whose aegis the wedding night begins, but the onset of evening also suggests that for all these resplendent figures, the day "is not long."

The final line of the refrain represents another form of closure, one less natural and more artful. More precisely, it sustains a perfectly modulated compact between art and nature:

"Sweete Themmes runne softly, till I end my Song." In this re-current appeal the Thames becomes a symbol of both nature and time, its "appointed tyde" (*Pro* 177) determining the hour of the wedding. It carries all we see on its flow—the nymphs and swans of Spenser's poetic reverie as well as the actual bridal party. Even London's "brickie towres / ... on Themmes brode aged backe doe ryde" (132–133), so that these seem-ingly solid and durable monuments rest not on firm ground but on the river's Heraclitean flux. Seen from this perspective, every "house of auncient fame" becomes more precariously situated. The noble names enshrined therein may prove as evanescent as the "Somers-heat." The *Prothalamion* achieves a perspective on all it encompasses comparable to the view in the "Mutability Cantos," but here time and nature align them-selves for the moment in a benign and gentle confluence under the poet's control. The moment only holds for the duration of the verse. Indeed, the poet's blend of exhortation and com-mand makes it hold: "Sweete Themmes runne softly, till I end my Song." The Thames, like the Lee, depends on the poet to articulate its otherwise mute significance. The poem and its undersong also comprehend and support all that we see therein, underwriting the fame of Essex, Elizabeth, and her court and holding them all in precarious accord. Spenser's vale-dictory refrain is a resonant affirmation of his song's enduring power over its own transient subjects.

Epilogue

In the summer of 1598 the Irish rose in rebellion against their English overlords, and Edmund Spenser was driven off his estate at Kilcolman Castle. He fled first to Cork and then to London, where he died in January 1599. He was buried, according to Camden, "at the chardge of the earl of Essex."[1] Essex was appointed Governor of Ireland the day after Spenser died, realizing one of the hopes set forth in *A View of the Present State of Ireland*; but his other hopes were disappointed. The Earl failed to suppress the uprising that had driven Spenser out, and he returned to England against orders. The heroic commander whose "prowesse and victorious armes" had promised to make "great Elisaes glorious name...ring through all the world" subsequently rebelled against her rule and died a traitor in 1601. In a sense, the *Prothalamion*'s scenes of chivalric glory and courtly harmony really did end when Spenser ended his song.

The heroes of Elizabethan chivalry lived on in a melancholy and nostalgic afterglow in the first decade of the next reign. Those writers who began their careers under Elizabeth and felt themselves, like Daniel, "the remnant of another time" (*Philotas*, p. 98) were especially fervent in their loyalty to these figures. Chapman's *Bussy D'Ambois* and his *Tragedy of Biron* were thought to allude sympathetically to Essex's downfall, and Fulke Greville destroyed his *Antony and Cleopatra* lest it be suspected of doing the same. Michael Drayton's *Poems Lyric and Pastoral*, published in 1606, depicted Sir Philip Sidney in heaven, "laughing even Kings and their delights to scorn."[2] Many of these writers pinned their hopes for the future on Henry, Prince of Wales, whose personal virtue, Protestant zeal, and military enthusiasms contrasted sharply with his father's deficiencies. Henry kept alive the dangerous image of chivalric magnificence and autonomy and "put forth himself in a more Heroicke manner than was usual with Princes of his Time, by Tiltings, Barriers, and other exercises on horsebacke, the Martial Discipline of gentle Peace, which caught the peoples eyes, and made their tongues the Messengers of their Hearts, in daily extolling his hopeful and gallant towardliness to admiration."[3] Ben Jonson and Inigo Jones devised two Arthurian entertainments for these occasions, *Prince Henry's Barriers* in 1610 and *Oberon* in 1611, the latter depicting the restoration of the House of Chivalry. Henry's death the next year shattered hopes for a revival of the chivalric compromise and deprived "the rites of knighthood" of their most ardent royal champion.

Nevertheless, the idea of "the rites of knighthood" continued to flourish. One of the most frequent participants in the chivalrous spectacles and tournaments favored by Prince Henry was Thomas Howard, the Earl of Arundel, who later became Earl Marshal.[4] Sir Robert Cotton's research on the office, undertaken for Arundel, persuaded King James to unite the Marshal's jurisdiction with the Constable's in 1622, and Cotton's successful endeavors represent the culmination of the inquiry initiated by the Earl of Essex in 1597. The Earl of Clarendon saw Arundel as a vain man obsessed with mere appearances: "He wore and affected a habit very different from that of the time, such as men had beheld in the pictures of most considerable men; all which drew the eyes of most, and the reverence of many, towards him, as the image and representative of the primitive nobility and native gravity of the nobles, when they had been most venerable. But this was only his outside, his nature and true humour being so much disposed to levity and vulgar delights." Rubens' portrait of Arundel in armor with his Marshal's baton and badge of Saint George certainly does create an impressive image of antique dignity, and even Clarendon concedes "that he had in his person, in his aspect and countenance, the appearance of a great man."[5] Yet for Arundel, preserving this image of venerable grandeur was essential to preserving the rights and privileges of his status, and he considered it his role as Earl Marshal to support the "ancient nobility and gentry, and to interpose on their behalfs."[6] As the government drifted toward civil war, Arundel, among others, advised the King to summon a Great Council of the peers to resolve the crisis.[7] Behind such proposals was an enduring belief in the constitutional authority of the ancient feudal offices and the superiority of a mixed government dominated by the aristocracy.

This persistent belief in the aristocracy's political preeminence and military authority inspired some noblemen to break with royal authority completely during the Civil War. Though most aristocrats sided with the crown, a few opposed Stuart rule in Parliament and in battle, at least at first. Indeed, some historians have argued that "the English civil war began as a rebellion led by what contemporaries called the greater and lesser nobility." The third Earl of Essex, son of the highborn "popular martyr" of Elizabethan chivalry, Robert Devereux, assumed command of a parliamentary army in 1642, and he exploited his father's enduring legend to rally various factions to fight for "the good old cause."[8] Aristocratic opposition was again justified by a belief in the superiority of mixed government. In a letter to Lord Wharton in 1657 Viscount Say declared, "The peers of England, and their power and privileges in the House of Lords, they have been as the beam keeping both scales, king and people, in an even posture, without encroachments one upon another to the hurt and damage of both. Long experience hath made it manifest that they have preserved the just rights and liberties of the people against the tyrannical usurpation of kings, and have also as steps and stairs upheld the Crown from falling and being cast down upon the floor by the insolency of the multitude from the throne of government."[9] The legends and ideals of Elizabethan chivalry combined with traditional notions of the ancient constitution to justify opposition to royal tyranny and assert "the just rights and liberties of the people."

Writing in defense of free speech in 1644, John Milton also drew inspiration from Elizabethan chivalry, but his sources were more literary. His *Areopagitica* contains an intriguing allusion to Daniel's *Civil Wars*. Daniel also compares books to the dragon's teeth of Cadmus, but the earlier poet condemns the printing press and gunpowder as infernal instruments of "Impious Contention" (*CW*, p. 216).[10] Nemesis instructs Pandora accordingly:

> Make new-borne Contradiction still to rise;
> As if Thebes-founder, Cadmus, tongues had sowne,
> In stead of teeth, for greater mutinies.
> Bring new-defended Faith, against Faith knowne;
> Weary the Soule with contrarieties;
> Till all Religion become retrograde,
> And that faire tire, the maske of sinne be made.
>
> (p. 216)

Milton completely reevaluates this image of self-destructive contention, making books "as lively, and as vigorously productive, as those fabulous Dragon's teeth...[which] being sown up and down, may chance to spring up armed men."[11] Less horrified than Daniel at the prospect of civil war, Milton is exhilarated by the notion of "armed" ideas. He is also more profoundly and positively inspired by Spenser's *Faerie Queene*, and, cheered by Spenser's chivalric ideal of *discordia concors*, embraces contrariety as a "brotherly dissimilitude" rather than fratricidal antagonism. Moreover, Milton's "trial by what is contrary" is a form of trial by combat, for which only "the true warfaring Christian" can be prepared.[12]

Milton's youthful literary ambitions were also fired by the legends of chivalric romance, as the yearnings expressed in *Manso* make clear: "If ever I shall summon back our native kings into our songs, and Arthur, waging his wars beneath the earth, or if ever I shall proclaim the magnanimous heroes of the table which their mutual fidelity made invincible, and (if only the spirit be with me) shall shatter the Saxon phalanxes under the British Mars!"[13] Nevertheless, *Paradise Lost*, his great epic of free will, draws on scripture rather than chivalric romance for inspiration. Moreover, despite his admiration for Spenser's heroes, Milton's own conception of heroism is clearly different. He ultimately prefers the "wayfaring" pilgrim to the "warfaring" knight, admiring courage in combat less than "the better fortitude / Of patience and heroic martyrdom." However, he still tells us that it was his early reading "among those lofty Fables and Romances, which recount in solemne cantos the deeds of Knighthood founded by our victorious Kings & from hence had in renowne over all Christendome," that taught him "that every free and gentle spirit...ought to be borne a Knight."[14] Long after the decline of its ceremonial forms—the swearing of oaths and "the laying of a sword"—the rights of knighthood were still equated, by Milton and many others, with the rights and liberties of "every free and gentle spirit."[15]

Notes

INTRODUCTION

1. William Shakespeare, *Richard II* I.i.75, in *The Riverside Shakespeare*, ed. G. Blakemore Evans (Boston: Houghton Mifflin, 1974), p. 806. All citations of Shakespeare are from this edition, hereafter cited in the text.

2. According to Stephen Booth, "the two words were not then differentiated by spelling," so the pun on rights and rites is a natural one. See his note to line 6 of Sonnet 23 in his edition of *Shakespeare's Sonnets* (New Haven: Yale University Press, 1977), p. 171.

3. *The Roxburghe Ballads*, ed. William Chapell (Hertford, 1888), 1: 564, 572.

4. Frances A. Yates, "Elizabethan Chivalry: The Romance of the Accession Day Tilts" in *Astraea: The Imperial Theme in the Sixteenth Century* (London: Routledge & Kegan Paul, 1975), pp. 88–111, and Roy Strong, *The Cult of Elizabeth* (London: Thames & Hudson, 1977), pp. 129–134 passim.

5. Sir Fulke Greville, "A Dedication to Sir Philip Sidney," in *The Prose Works of Fulke Greville, Lord Brooke*, ed. John Gouws (Oxford: Clarendon Press, 1985), p. 41.

6. Kenneth Burke, *The Philosophy of Literary Form* (1941; Berkeley and Los Angeles: University of California Press, 1973), pp. 8–9, and *A Grammar of Motives* (1945; New York: Prentice-Hall, 1952), p. 447; Clifford Geertz, "Deep Play: Notes on the Balinese Cockfight," in *The Interpretation of Cultures* (New York: Basic Books, 1973), p. 440; Fredric Jameson, *The Political Unconscious: Narrative as a Socially Symbolic Act* (Ithaca: Cornell University Press, 1980), p. 80.

7. Samuel Daniel, *The Civil Wars*, ed. Laurence Michel (New Haven: Yale University Press, 1958), pp. 72, 312; Sir Philip Sidney, *An Apology for Poetry*, ed. Geoffrey Shepherd (1965; Manchester: Manchester University Press, 1973), p. 104; "A Letter of the Avthors to Sir Walter Raleigh," in *The Poetical Works of Edmund Spenser*, ed. J. C. Smith and E. De Selincourt (1912; London: Oxford

University Press, 1965), pp. 407–408. All references to Spenser's poetry are to this edition, and the major works are cited in the text.

8. See Kenneth Burke, "Literature as Equipment for Living" in *The Philosophy of Literary Form*, pp. 293–304.

9. Burke, *Philosophy of Literary Form*, p. 298.

10. Kenneth Burke, *Attitudes Towards History* (1937: Los Altos, Calif.: Hermes Publications, 1959), p. 92.

11. Stephen Greenblatt, *Renaissance Self-Fashioning: From More to Shakespeare* (Chicago: University of Chicago Press, 1980), p. 8. According to Greenblatt, subversion is generally "contained by the power it would appear to threaten. Indeed the subversiveness is the very product of the power and furthers its ends." This is the argument Greenblatt advances in *Shakespearean Negotiations: The Circulation of Social Energy in Renaissance England* (Berkeley and Los Angeles: University of California Press, 1988), p. 30.

12. *Attitudes Towards History*, p. 20.

13. Fredric Jameson, "Critical Response: Ideology and Symbolic Action," *Critical Inquiry* 5 (1978): 422.

14. Jonathan Goldberg, *Voice Terminal Echo: Postmodernism and English Renaissance Texts* (New York: Methuen, 1986), p. 49.

15. J. E. Neale, *Elizabeth I and Her Parliaments, 1584–1601* (1958; New York: Norton, 1966), p. 436.

16. John Milton, *Areopagitica*, ed. Ernest Sirluck, in *Complete Prose Works* (New Haven: Yale University Press, 1959), 2:515. "Wayfaring" appears in the first edition of the text, but the change to "warfaring" is generally thought to be authoritative. See Sirluck's note on this passage, 2:515n.102.

CHAPTER 1

1. Samuel Daniel, "Epistle Dedicatory to the Collection of the History of England" (1626) in *The Complete Works*, ed. Alexander B. Grosart (1896; New York, Russell & Russell, 1963), 4:77; Lawrence Stone, *The Crisis of the Aristocracy, 1588–1641* (Oxford: Clarendon Press, 1965).

2. Penry Williams, *The Tudor Regime* (Oxford: Clarendon Press, 1979), p. 436. Williams contends that the "royal monopoly of violence" was less complete than Stone claims (p. 436 n.26).

3. Malcolm Vale, *War and Chivalry* (London: Duckworth, 1981), p. 79. The aristocracy's chivalric notion of duty and vocation was incorporated, in Vale's view, into a "Renaissance cult of fame" (p. 78).

4. Sir Robert Naunton, *Fragmenta Regalia* (Washington, D.C.: Folger Books, 1985), ed. John S. Cerovski, p. 36. Hereafter cited in the text.

5. Richard Bagwell, *Ireland Under the Tudors* (London, 1885–1890), 2:210, 209, 234.

6. Roy E. Schreiber, *The Political Career of Sir Robert Naunton, 1589–1635* (London: Royal Historical Society, 1981), p. 3.

7. John Cerovski recounts Naunton's career in his introduction to *Fragmenta Regalia*, pp. 13–30. According to Roy Schreiber, his final years were shadowed by disgrace and a fall from political power (*Sir Robert Naunton*, pp. 114ff.).

8. M. Jacques Hurault, *Politicke, Moral and Martial Discourses*, trans. Arthur Golding (London, 1595), p. 287. Hurault distinguishes magnanimity from prowess "in that prowesse respecteth chiefly the perils of warre, and magnanimitie respecteth honour," but he concludes that, generally, "magnanimitie and prowess agree" (p. 287).

9. Sir William Segar, *Honor, Military and Civil* (1602), ed. Diane Bornstein (Delmar, N. Y.: Scholars' Facsimiles and Reprints, 1975), p. 210.

10. Aristotle, *Ethics (The Nicomachean Ethics)*, trans. J. A. K. Thomson (1955; Harmondsworth: Penguin, 1977) pp. 157, 68.

11. Francis Markham, *The Booke of Honour or Five Decades of Epistles of Honour* (London, 1625), p. 4. Segar takes the same line in *Honor, Military and Civil*, p. 210.

12. Robert Glover, "Of Nobility Political and Civill," p. 26, and Thomas Milles, "Peroration," sig. K 5r, in Glover, *The Catalogue of Honor*, trans. Thomas Milles (London, 1610).

13. Ibid., p. 1. The first would include peerages; the second, knighthoods.

14. Ibid.

15. William Huse Dunham, "William Camden's Commonplace Book," *The Yale University Library Gazette* 43 (1969): 147. Dunham notes that an English nobleman could not disclaim his ennobled blood until an act of Parliament allowed him to do so in 1963.

16. Glover, *Catalogue of Honor*, p. 77.

17. Mervyn James, "English Politics and the Concept of Honour, 1485–1642," in *Society, Politics, and Culture: Studies in Early Modern England* (Cambridge: Cambridge University Press, 1986), pp. 308–415.

18. Vale, *War and Chivalry*, p. 99.

19. Richard Rawlinson, *The History of That Most Eminent Statesman, Sir John Perrott* (London, 1728), p. 29.

20. College of Arms Score Cheques, fol. 8r, 23r.

21. Rawlinson, *Sir John Perrot*, p. 48; see also Henry Machyn, *Diary*, ed. John Gough Nichols (London, 1848), p. 203.

22. Rawlinson, *Sir John Perrot*, p. 49.

23. Yates, *Astraea*, p. 97.

24. Anthony Esler, *The Aspiring Mind of the Elizabethan Younger Generation* (Durham: Duke University Press, 1966), p. 115; Arthur B. Ferguson, *The Indian Summer of English Chivalry* (Durham: Duke University Press, 1960), pp. 125, 103; Ferguson, *The Chivalric Tradition in Renaissance England* (Washington: Folger Books, 1986), pp. 11, 97, 138; William Schofield, *Chivalry in English Literature: Chaucer, Malory, Spenser and Shakespeare* (1912; Port Washington, N.Y.: Kennikat Press, 1964), p. 3. Schofield, in turn, cites and draws on the work of Leon Gautier and John Addington Symonds.

25. Yates, *Astraea*, p. 101. Strong, *Cult of Elizabeth*, p. 161.

26. Roy Strong, *Splendor at Court: Renaissance Spectacle and the Theater of Power* (Boston: Houghton Mifflin, 1973), pp. 37–38. In an updated version of this work, entitled *Art and Power: Renaissance Festivals, 1450–1650* (Woodbridge: Boydell Press, 1984), Strong remarks on the tournament's value as "training for war" (p. 12), but he still contends that tournaments were carefully "stage-managed to ensure that the monarch or heir apparent was always the victor" and thus designed as "a standard vehicle for expressing princely magnificence" (p. 50). Alan Young takes the same line in his recent study, arguing that Elizabeth used "the tournament as an instrument of propaganda to her maximum advantage" (*Tudor and Jacobean Tournaments* [London: George Philip, 1987], p. 32).

27. Ramon Lull, *The Book of the Ordre of Chyvalry*, trans. William Caxton, ed. Alfred T. P. Byles (London: Early English Text Society, Oxford University Press, 1926), pp. 2, 38–39, 32, 19.

28. J. E. A. Jolliffe, *The Constitutional History of Medieval England* (1937; London: Adam and Charles Black, 1961), p. 424.

29. Larry D. Benson, *Malory's Morte Darthur* (Cambridge, Mass.: Harvard University Press, 1976), p. 143.

30. Maurice Keen, *Chivalry* (New Haven: Yale University Press, 1984), p. 247.

31. Vale, *War and Chivalry*, pp. 165, 174.

32. Keen, *Chivalry*, p. 239, 249.

33. Wallace MacCaffrey, *The Shaping of the Elizabethan Regime* (1968; Princeton: Princeton University Press, 1972), pp. 99–100.

34. Sir Francis Bacon, *The Essayes or Counsells, Civill and Morall,*

ed. Michael Kiernan (Cambridge, Mass.: Harvard University Press, 1985), p. 41.

35. Neville Williams, *Thomas Howard, Fourth Duke of Norfolk* (London: Barrie and Rochliff, 1964), p. 48.

36. J. E. Neale, "The Elizabethan Political Scene," in *Essays in Elizabethan History* (London: Jonathan Cape, 1958), p. 70.

37. See Vale's chapter on orders of chivalry in the fifteenth century, in Vale, *War and Chivalry*, pp. 33–62, and Strong's chapter on the Order of the Garter in *Cult of Elizabeth*, pp. 164–185.

38. Elias Ashmole describes James's efforts to prohibit "Livery Coats" and reduce the number of attendants at Garter ceremonies in *The Institution, Laws and Ceremonies of the Most Noble Order of the Garter* (London, 1672), p. 339.

39. *Burkes Peerage*, ed. L. G. Pine (London: Burkes Peerage, 1959), p. 1688. Ashmole also provides a description of this "glorious show" (*Order of the Garter*, pp. 339–340).

40. Strong, *Cult of Elizabeth*, p. 112.

41. John Ferne, *The Blazon of Gentrie* (London, 1586), p. 120.

42. Edward Maunde Thompson, "The Revision of the Statutes of the Order of the Garter by King Edward the Sixth," *Archaeologia* 54 (1894): 184.

43. Thomas Milles, "Peroration," in Glover, *Catalogue of Honor*, sig. K 5r.

44. See Lupold von Wedel's contemporary description in "The Journey Through England Made by Lupold von Wedel in the Years 1584 and 1585," trans. Gottfried von Bülow, *Transactions of the Royal Historical Society*, n.s., 9 (1895): 258–259.

45. *Historical Manuscripts Commission, Salisbury* (London: HMSO, 1904), 10:385.

46. College of Arms, MS M.6, fol. 56r. I discuss this manuscript and its links to Robert Dudley in greater detail in the next chapter.

47. Sir John Harington prints the rules in *Nugae Antiquae*, ed. Henry Harington (London, 1779), 3:234–239.

48. Sydney Anglo, "Archives of the English Tournament: Score Cheques and Lists," *Journal of the Society of Archivists* 2 (1962): 157–158.

49. Ibid.

50. Ibid., p. 158.

51. George Peele, *Polyhymnia*, in *The Life and Minor Works*, ed. David H. Horne (New Haven: Yale University Press, 1952), 1:241.

52. Peele, *Anglorum Feriae*, in *Works*, 1:273.

53. Sir William Segar, "Feast of St. George Observed at Utrecht, 1586," in *The Progresses and Public Processions of Queen Elizabeth*, ed. J. Nichols (London, 1823), 2:457.

54. Michael Walzer, *The Revolution of the Saints* (1965; New York: Atheneum, 1976), p. 272. Walzer is quoting Castiglione.

55. Alan Young, *Tudor and Jacobean Tournaments*, p. 90.

56. College of Arms, MS M6, fol. 62r. Alan Young says the number could run as high as twelve thousand (pp. 75–76).

57. Geertz, *Interpretation of Cultures*, p. 436, 440, 443.

58. Baldesar Castiglione, *The Book of the Courtier*, trans. Charles S. Singleton (Garden City, N.Y.: Doubleday, 1959), p. 165.

59. Geertz, *Interpretation of Cultures*, p. 443.

60. Kenneth Burke, *Philosophy of Literary Form*, p. 89.

61. See the "Editor's Note" to *Vindiciae Contra Tyrannos*, in *Constitutionalism and Resistance in the Sixteenth Century: Three Treatises by Hotman, Beza, and Mornay*, ed. and trans. Julian H. Franklin (New York: Pegasus, 1969), p. 139.

62. Walzer, *Revolution of the Saints*, p. 73.

63. *Vindiciae Contra Tyrannos*, pp. 191–192.

64. The source for this information is the collection of score cheques in the College of Arms; Roy Strong prints lists of the participants in the Accession Day tilts and St. Elizabeth's Day tilts (November 19), from 1581 to 1602, in *The Cult of Elizabeth*, pp. 206–212. Compton became the Earl of Northampton, and it was his magnificent Garter ceremony that earned him the Order's "vote of thanks" (see note 39).

Chapter 2

1. College of Arms, MS M6, fol. 57v.

2. Edward Hall, *The Union of the Two Noble Families of Lancaster and York*, ed. H. Ellis (London, 1809), pp. 689–690.

3. See Sydney Anglo's description of Henry VIII's unruly coronation tournament, in *The Great Tournament Roll of Westminster* (Oxford: Clarendon Press, 1968), [2]: 49.

4. Hall, *Union of the Two Noble Families*, p. 689.

5. David M. Loades, *The Tudor Court* (London: Batsford, 1986), p. 103.

6. Hall, *Union of the Two Noble Families*, pp. 707–708.

7. See Anglo, *Spectacle, Pageantry, and Early Tudor Policy* (Oxford: Clarendon Press, 1969), p. 73.

8. See Barrett L. Beer, *Northumberland: The Political Career of John Dudley, Earl of Warwick and Duke of Northumberland* (Kent, Ohio: Kent State University Press, 1973), pp. 12–13. Beer concludes that John Dudley was "above all else a soldier and a courtier" (p. 13).

9. Anglo, *Spectacle*, pp. 303–304.

10. *The Chronicle and Political Papers of King Edward VI*, ed. W. K. Jordan (London: Allen & Unwin, 1966), pp. 31–32, 97, 103, 105–106.

11. For a more complete discussion of the circumstances of the Dudleys' release from prison, the tournament that followed, and the somewhat confusing records of the event, see my "From the Tower to the Tiltyard: Robert Dudley's Return to Glory," *The Historical Journal* 27 (1984): 425–435.

12. *Calendar of State Papers, Spanish*, Philip and Mary (1554–1558), ed. Royal Tyler (London: HMSO, 1916), 13:60–61.

13. Frances A. Yates, *The Valois Tapestries* (1959; London: Routledge & Kegan Paul, 1975), p. 54.

14. College of Arms, MS M6, fol. 41v.

15. John Neale, *Queen Elizabeth* (1934; Garden City, N. Y.: Anchor Books, 1957), p. 78.

16. *CSP, Spanish*, Elizabeth (1558-1567), ed. Martin A. S. Hume (London, 1892), 1:113–114.

17. William Camden, *Annales, or the History of the Most Renowned and Victorious Princess Elizabeth*, trans. R. Norton (London, 1635), p. 64.

18. *CSP, Spanish*, Elizabeth, 1:113.

19. Williams, *Thomas Howard*, pp. 41–42.

20. Ibid., pp. 42–43, and Anthony Wagner, *The Records and Collections of the College of Arms* (London: Burkes Peerage, 1952), p. 12.

21. Sir Anthony Wagner, *Heralds of England: A History of the Office and College of Arms* (London: HMSO, 1967), p. 197. Norfolk's Orders of 1568 are printed in Joseph Edmondson, *A Complete Body of Heraldry* (London, 1780), 1:143–147.

22. The volume is included in a case of books and items associated with Mary, Queen of Scots, at the Isabella Stewart Gardner Museum; see David Starkey, "Stewart Serendipity: A Missing Text of the *Modus Tenendi Parliamentum*," in *Fenway Court* (Boston: Isabella Stewart Gardner Museum, 1986), p. 39.

23. Nicholas Pronay and John Taylor, *Parliamentary Texts of the Later Middle Ages* (Oxford: Clarendon, 1980), pp. 20–21.

24. Ibid., p. 87.

25. L. W. Vernon-Harcourt, *His Grace the Steward and the Trial of Peers* (London: Longmans, Green, 1907), pp. 143–147. See also Pronay and Taylor, who cite arguments for and against the validity of parliamentary deposition of Edward II (*Parliamentary Texts*, 96). The *Modus* is ambiguous, insisting on the need for agreement between King and council even when they disagree (pp. 87–88).

26. Pronay and Taylor, *Parliamentary Texts*, pp. 56–57.

27. Starkey, "Stewart Serendipity," p. 49.

28. Camden, *Annales*, p. 114.

29. BL Add. MS 15091 and 38139. I am indebted to David Starkey and Simon Adams for informing me of this fact.

30. Wagner, *Heralds of England*, p. 209. Wagner attributes the squabbles among the heralds during this period to Shrewsbury's "indifferent" leadership.

31. Ibid., p. 199.

32. Lawrence Stone, *The Causes of the English Revolution, 1529–1642* (London: Routledge & Kegan Paul, 1972), p. 72.

33. Machyn, *Diary*, pp. 275–276. I am grateful to Simon Adams for calling this reference to my attention.

34. W. Godfrey, A. Wagner, and H. Stanford London, *Sixteenth Monograph of the London Survey Committee* (London: College of Arms, 1963), p. 84, and Wagner, *Heralds of England*, p. 209.

35. Wagner, *Heralds of England*, p. 216, 207, 209.

36. College of Arms, MS L9. The common ancestor is Raffe Neville, Earl of Westmoreland.

37. Dudley Papers, Longleat, MS 149b, fol. 10r. The pedigree was drawn up in 1583 and includes Leicester's son Robert, the "noble imp," who died the next year.

38. College of Arms, MS M6, fols. 56v–57r.

39. See my "Tower to the Tiltyard," pp. 432–435. Sir Anthony Wagner graciously helped me to make these tentative identifications.

40. College of Arms, MS M6, fol. 59v. The original is included among the tournament score cheques, fol. 67r.

41. Anglo, "Archives of the English Tournament," p. 155.

42. Marie Axton, "Robert Dudley and the Inner Temple Revels," *The Historical Journal* 13 (1970): 365.

43. Gerard Legh, *Accedens of Armorie* (London, 1562). Legh's narrative takes the form of a dream vision, making it hard to say which events actually occurred and which are fictional interpolations.

44. Anglo, *Spectacle*, pp. 120–121.

45. Axton, "Dudley and the Inner Temple," 367–368.

46. John Guillim, *A Display of Heraldrie* (London, 1610), a.2v.

47. Frank Whigham, *Ambition and Privilege: The Social Tropes of Elizabethan Courtesy Theory* (Berkeley and Los Angeles: University of California Press, 1984), pp. 5–6, 18–19.

48. John Ferne dedicates *The Blazon of Gentry* to the Gentlemen of the Inner Temple, braving the censure from above of "professed Armorists" for revealing their secrets and of their patrons, who stand on "the vaine ostentation of noblenes and bloud," as well as attacks from below by commoners and their "new conceited Blazonners" (a.5v–a.6r). He presents himself as the true defender of virtue and social hierarchy. If the gentility of the Inns of Court went unrecognized by the College of Arms, it could be defiantly publicized by one of their own.

49. *CSP, Spanish*, Elizabeth, 1:404.

50. John Leland, *De Rebus Collectanea*, ed. T. Hearne (London, 1770), 2:668.

51. See Winfried Schleiner, "*Divina Virago*: Queen Elizabeth as an Amazon," *Studies in Philology* 75 (1978): 179–180. Marie Axton has described a number of entertainments associated with Leicester during this period that carry their endorsement of marriage to almost insulting lengths. A wedding masque written by Thomas Pound, for example, declares the bride more beautiful than the Queen because the bride fulfills her destiny in marriage; see Marie Axton, *The Queen's Two Bodies* (London: Royal Historical Society, 1977), pp. 51–56.

52. *CSP, Spanish*, Elizabeth, 1:518, 461, 575.

53. George Gascoigne, *The Complete Works* (Cambridge: Cambridge University Press, 1910), 2:119. "The Princely Pleasures of Kenilworth" appeared in an early edition of Gascoigne's works in 1587.

54. Robert Langham, *A Letter* (1575), ed. R. J. P. Kuin (Leiden: E. J. Brill, 1983), pp. 40–41. For a discussion of the authorship of this text and the controversy surrounding it, see David Scott, "William Patten and the Authorship of Robert Laneham's *Letter* (1575)" *English Literary Renaissance* 7 (1977): 297–306.

55. Gascoigne, *Works*, 2:99.

56. Gascoigne, *Works*, 2:100, and Langham, *Letter*, p. 46.

57. Langham, *Letter*, p. 46. Gascoigne makes no mention of the incident, but Langham makes sport of this and several other mishaps; his mocking tone may have prompted the suppression of his tract (see Scott, "Laneham's *Letter*," p. 297 and pp. 301–302).

58. Gascoigne, *Works*, 2:120, 123.

59. Richard C. McCoy, "Gascoigne's *Poëmata Castrata*: The Wages of Courtly Success," *Criticism* 27 (1985): 29–54.

60. "The Queen's Majesty's entertainment at Woodstock," ed. A. W. Pollard (1903; Oxford: H. Daniel and H. Hart, 1910), p. xxviii.

61. Naunton, *Fragmenta Regalia*, p. 41.

62. Loades, *Tudor Court*, p. 145.

63. Quoted in Derek Wilson, *Sweet Robin* (London: Hamish Hamilton, 1981), p. 176.

64. *CSP, Spanish*, Elizabeth, 1:512.

65. William Dugdale, *The Antiquities of Warwick and Warwick Castle* (Warwick, 1786), pp. 141–143. See Alan Kendall's account of this event and the Earl's anger at the townspeople of Warwick for failing to pay their respects on time, in *Robert Dudley, Earl of Leicester* (London: Cassell, 1980), pp. 134–137.

66. Charles Wilson, *Queen Elizabeth and the Revolt of the Netherlands* (London: Macmillan, 1970), p. 89.

67. Wallace MacCaffrey, *Queen Elizabeth and the Making of Policy, 1572–1588* (Princeton: Princeton University Press, 1981), p. 352.

68. Roy Strong and Jan Van Dorsten, *Leicester's Triumph* (Leiden: Leiden University Press, 1964), pp. 84–85.

69. *The Correspondence of Robert Dudley, Earl of Leycester, during his Government of the Low Countries, 1585–86*, ed. J. Bruce (London, 1844), December 26, 1585, p. 32.

70. *CSP, Foreign*, Elizabeth (1585–1586), ed. Sophie Crawford Lomas (London: HMSO, 1921), 20:67.

71. Raphael Holinshed, *Chronicles of England, Scotland, and Ireland* (1808; New York: AMS Press, 1965), p. 643.

72. Strong and Van Dorsten, *Leicester's Triumph*, pp. 37–38 and Holinshed, *Chronicles*, p. 646.

73. *CSP, Foreign*, Elizabeth, 20:320.

74. Leicester, *Correspondence*, February 11, 1586, pp. 111–114.

75. Ibid., February 10, 1585/6, pp. 110, 106–107.

76. Ibid., March 9, 1586, pp. 163–164.

77. Ibid., April 1, 1586, p. 209.

78. Holinshed, *Chronicles*, p. 658.

79. Leicester, *Correspondence*, July 29, 1586, p. 367.

80. Charles Wilson, *Queen Elizabeth and the Revolt*, p. 99. But see Simon Adams's revisionist account of this episode, "A Patriot for Whom: Stanley, York and Elizabeth's Catholics," *History Today* 37 (July 1987): 46–50.

81. Charles Wilson, *Queen Elizabeth and the Revolt*, pp. 99–100, and MacCaffrey, *Queen Elizabeth and the Making of Policy*, p. 359.

82. Leicester, *Correspondence*, April 5, 1586, p. 215.

83. F. J. Levy, "Philip Sidney Reconsidered," *English Literary Renaissance* 2 (1972): 15. Katherine Duncan-Jones examines Walsingham's plight in *Miscellaneous Prose of Sir Philip Sidney*, ed. Katherine Duncan-Jones and Jan Van Dorsten (Oxford: Clarendon Press, 1973), p. 143. Cooke's role in Sidney's funeral procession is noted in Thomas Lant's roll, *Sequitur celebritas & pompa funeris* (London, 1587), fol. 2r.

84. Kendall, *Robert Dudley*, p. 226. See Leicester's rejoinder in Strong and Van Dorsten, *Leicester's Triumph*, p. 8. The medal he commissioned said, "I do not leave the herd, but the ungrateful ones" (Strong and Van Dorsten, p. 77).

85. Camden, *Annales*, p. 356.

86. John Clapham, *Elizabeth of England* (1603), ed. Evelyn Plummer Read and Conyers Read (Philadelphia: University of Pennsylvania Press, 1951), p. 91.

87. Camden, *Annales*, pp. 145–146.

88. Dudley Papers, Longleat, box 3, f. 62.

89. Miller Christy, "Queen Elizabeth's Visit to Tilbury in 1588," *English Historical Review* 34 (1919): 45.

90. *CSP, Domestic*, Elizabeth (1581–1590), ed. Robert Lemon (London, 1865), 2:509, 515.

91. Derek Wilson, *Sweet Robin*, p. 299.

92. Neale, *Queen Elizabeth*, p. 309.

93. James Aske, *Elizabetha Triumphans* (1588; facsimile, Amsterdam: Da Capo Press, 1969), p. 21.

94. Pepys, MS 2503 (State Papers II), fol. 403r–403v. This was his second will, an earlier one having been drafted in 1582.

95. Ibid., fol. 394r.

96. J. Payne Collier, "Documents, etc. regarding Sir Walter Raleigh," *Notes and Queries*, 3d series, 5 (1864): 109.

97. Thomas Rogers, *Leicester's Ghost* (1605), ed. Franklin B. Williams (Chicago: Newberry Library and University of Chicago Press, 1972). See *Leicester's Commonwealth* (1584), ed. D. C. Peck (Athens, Ohio: Ohio University Press, 1985), p. 227 n. 4.

98. "'News from Heaven and Hell': A Defamatory Narrative of the Earl of Leicester," ed. D. C. Peck, *English Literary Renaissance* 8 (1978): 157.

99. MacCaffrey, *Queen Elizabeth and the Making of Policy*, p. 441, 444–445.

CHAPTER 3

1. Malcolm William Wallace, *The Life of Sir Philip Sidney* (Cambridge: Cambridge University Press, 1915), p. 69.

2. *HMC, De L'Isle and Dudley*, ed. C. L. Kingsford (London: HMSO, 1925), 1:304.

3. See D. C. Peck's introduction to *Leicester's Commonwealth*, showing its influence on more respectable histories such as Camden's, Naunton's, Ashmole's, and others (p. 45).

4. *Leicester's Commonwealth*, pp. 80, 174.

5. Sidney, *Defence of the Earl of Leicester*, in *Miscellaneous Prose*, p. 140.

6. Ibid., p. 134.

7. Ibid., p. 135. Cooke's genealogy also includes, in addition to Guy of Warwick, these same families as in Dudley's family tree (Dudley Papers, Longleat, MS 149b).

8. Sidney, *Defence of the Earl of Leicester*, p. 140.

9. Peck argues that the author was not Robert Parsons, as is generally assumed, but Charles Arundel, with the assistance of others in the Catholic court party (*Leicester's Commonwealth*, p. 25–32).

10. Sidney, *The Lady of May*, in *Miscellaneous Prose*, pp. 30–31.

11. William Ringler discusses the connection between military aid to the Dutch and the *Lady of May* in his edition of *The Poems of Sir Philip Sidney* (1962; Oxford: Clarendon Press, 1967), p. 362.

12. "A Letter Written by Sir Philip Sidney to Queen Elizabeth, Touching Her Marriage with Monsieur," in *Miscellaneous Prose*, p. 48.

13. Ibid., pp. 46, 54.

14. In her introduction to this letter in *Miscellaneous Prose* Katherine Duncan-Jones insists on the tact and intelligence of Sidney's letter and accurately notes the lack of evidence for his "banishment" from court (pp. 35–36). I find her contention that the letter "may have given little or no offence" (p. 36) less persuasive. Elizabeth raged at her Privy Council for addressing the subject, and Sidney's marginal status at court would only have made his advice seem more presumptuous rather than less.

15. Greville, *Prose Works*, pp. 40–41.

16. Ibid., p. 41, 87.

17. Ephim G. Fogel argues that Sidney is probably the author of most of the challengers' speeches, in "A Possible Addition to the Sidney Canon," *Modern Language Notes* 75 (1960): 389–394.

18. Sidney, *The Four Foster Children of Desire*, in *Entertainments for*

Elizabeth I (Totawa, N.J.: Brewer, Rowman, and Littlefield, 1980), ed. Jean Wilson, p. 70; hereafter cited in the text.

19. These are included by Ringler as "Poems possibly by Sidney" 4 and 5, in Sidney, *Poems*, pp. 345–346.

20. See Norman Council, "*O Dea Certe*: The Allegory of the Fortress of Perfect Beauty," *Huntington Library Quarterly* 39 (1976): 334.

21. Naunton, *Fragmenta Regalia*, p. 75. See also Arthur Marotti's discussion of desire as a trope for ambition, and grace as a trope for patronage, in "'Love Is Not Love:' Elizabethan Sonnet Sequences and the Social Order," *ELH* 49 (1982): 396–428.

22. Bacon, "Discourse in Praise of the Queen," in *Works*, ed. James Spedding, Robert Leslie Ellis, and Douglas Denon Heath (1857–1874; New York: Garrett Press, 1968), 8:139, and "In Felicem Memoriam Elizabethae," in *Works*, 6:317.

23. Louis Adrian Montrose, "Celebration and Insinuation: Sir Philip Sidney and the Motives of Elizabethan Courtship," *Renaissance Drama*, n.s., 8 (1977): 3–35.

24. Christopher Marlowe, *Edward II*, II.ii.34–35, in *The Complete Works of Christopher Marlowe*, ed. Fredson Bowers (1973; Cambridge University Press, 1981), p. 39.

25. Camden, *Remaines* (1605), p. 174, cited by Ringler in Sidney, *Poems*, p. 441.

26. "Correspondence," November 13, 1581, in *The Prose Works of Sir Philip Sidney*, ed. Albert Feuillerat (1912; Cambridge: Cambridge University Press, 1969), 3:138.

27. Ibid., December 28, 1581, p. 140.

28. Wallace, *Life of Sir Philip Sidney*, p. 273.

29. Sidney, *Astrophil and Stella* 30, in *Poems*, p. 180.

30. Marotti, "Love Is Not Love," p. 406. At the same time, Marotti contends that Sidney continues to address courtly issues of patronage and ambition throughout the sequence.

31. Annabel Patterson, *Censorship and Interpretation* (Madison: University of Wisconsin Press, 1984), p. 41.

32. A. C. Hamilton, *Sir Philip Sidney: A Study of His Life and Works* (Cambridge: Cambridge University Press, 1977), pp. 21, 17.

33. Sidney, *Poems*, p. 35.

34. Ibid., pp. 262–264. Ringler dates them after 1581 (p. 498); they were published in 1602.

35. Peter Beal, "Poems by Sir Philip Sidney: The Ottley Manuscript," *The Library* 33 (1978): 284–295. Beal proposes both 1577 and 1583 as possible dates of composition since Elizabeth's Acces-

sion Day fell on a Sunday, the "sabaoth" referred to in the dedication; but there is no record of Sidney jousting in 1583.

36. Sir Philip Sidney, *The Countess of Pembroke's Arcadia (The Old Arcadia)*, ed. Jean Robertson (Oxford: Clarendon Press, 1973), p. 159; hereafter cited in the text.

37. Greville, *Prose Works*, p. 38.

38. Emma Marshall Denkinger, "The *Impresa* Portrait of Sir Philip Sidney in the National Portrait Gallery," *PMLA* 47 (1932): 17.

39. Sidney, *Apology for Poetry*, p. 99.

40. Sidney, *The "New" Arcadia* (1590), in *Prose Works*, 1:282–283; hereafter cited in the text.

41. Yates, *Astraea*, pp. 88–90.

42. See Malcolm Parkinson, "Sidney's Portrayal of Mounted Combat with Lances," in *Spenser Studies* (New York: AMS Press, 1984), 5:231–251.

43. David Norbrook, *Poetry and Politics in the English Renaissance* (London: Routledge & Kegan Paul, 1984), p. 106.

44. For a discussion of the influence of Huguenot theories of the subaltern magistrate on Sidney's thought, see William D. Briggs, "Political Ideas in Sidney's *Arcadia*," *Studies in Philology* 28 (1931): 137–161, and my own *Sir Philip Sidney: Rebellion in Arcadia* (New Brunswick, N.J.: Rutgers University Press, 1979), pp. 8–11, 183–186. In *Faire Bitts: Sir Philip Sidney and Renaissance Political Theory* (Pittsburgh: Duquesne University Press, 1984) Martin N. Raitiere attributes the *Vindiciae* to Hubert Languet, Sidney's friend and mentor (pp. 113–141), and he concludes that Sidney repudiates the radicalism of the work (pp. 103–110). For a more comprehensive account of Huguenot theory, see J. W. Allen, *A History of Political Thought in the Sixteenth Century* (1928; London: Methuen, 1957), pp. 302–331, and Walzer, *Revolution of the Saints*, pp. 74–87. The major documents are included in Julian Franklin, ed., *Constitutionalism and Resistance in the Sixteenth Century*.

45. Sidney, "Correspondence," January 27, 1583, in *Prose Works*, 3:143.

46. Greville, *Prose Works*, p. 46.

47. Sidney, "Correspondence," March 24, 1586, in *Prose Works*, 3:166, 167.

48. Greville, *Prose Works*, p. 72.

49. Edmund Molyneux, "Memoir," in Holinshed, *Chronicles*, p. 1552. See also John Gouws's commentary on Greville's *Dedication* in Greville, *Prose Works*, pp. 212–213.

50. Sidney, "Correspondence," February 12, 1586, in *Prose Works*, 3:160.

51. Ibid., August 14, 1586, 3:179, 180.

52. Simon Adams, "The Military Campaign of 1586," paper presented at the International Conference on Sir Philip Sidney, Leiden, The Netherlands, September 2–4, 1986. The Netherlands war was, as J. R. Hale says, "largely a war of sieges." See J. R. Hale, *The Art of War and Renaissance England* (Washington, D.C.: Folger Press, 1961), p. 26.

53. *CSP, Foreign*, Elizabeth (1586–1587), ed. Sophie Crawford Lomas and Allen B. Hinds (London: HMSO, 1927), 21(ii): 165.

54. *The Correspondence of Sir Philip Sidney and Hubert Languet*, trans. Stuart A. Pears (London, 1845), p. 137.

55. George Whetstone, *Sir Philip Sidney, his valiant death, and true vertues* (1586), sig. C 1v.

56. Greville, *Prose Works*, p. 76. Sir John Smythe contends, on the other hand, that Sidney charged without leg armor because he was one of the "new fantasied men of war ... [who] despise and scorn our ancient arming of ourselves both on horseback and on foot, saying that we armed ourselves in times past with too much armor," in his *Certain Discourses Military*, ed. J. R. Hale (Ithaca: Cornell University Press, 1964), p. 42.

57. Greville, *Prose Works*, p. 77

58. Thomas Moffet, *Nobilis or A View of the Life and Death Of a Sidney (and Lessus Lugubris)*, trans. Virgil B. Heltzel and Hoyt H. Hudson (San Marino, Calif: Huntington Library Press, 1940), pp. 90, 93.

59. Ludovico Ariosto, *Orlando Furioso*, trans. Barbara Reynolds (1975; Harmondsworth, England: Penguin, 1977), pp. 350–351, and Miguel de Cervantes, *Don Quixote*, trans. J. M. Cohen (1950; Harmondsworth, England: Penguin, 1978), p. 344.

60. Arthur Golding, "Epistle Dedicatorie," in Philippe de Mornay, *A Woorke Concerning the Trewenesse of the Christian Religion* (London, 1587), pp. 3*v, 4*r.

61. Greville, *Prose Works*, p. 89. Compare Greville's claim that "in the whole course of his life he did so constantly balance ambition with safe precepts of divine and moral duty as no pretence whatsoever could have enticed that gentleman to break through the circle of a good patriot" (p. 75).

62. John Phillips, *The Life and Death of Sir Philip Sidney* (London, 1587), sig. B 2v.

63. Yates, *Astraea*, p. 103; Greenblatt, *Renaissance Self-Fashioning*, p. 256.

64. Peele, *Polyhymnia* (1590), in *Works*, 1:235–236.

65. Strong, *Cult of Elizabeth*, p. 140.

CHAPTER 4

1. Camden, *Annales*, p. 553.

2. Robert Lacey, *Robert, Earl of Essex* (New York: Atheneum, 1971), p. 35.

3. Walter Bourchier Devereux, *Lives and Letters of the Devereux, Earls of Essex* (London, 1853), 1:178.

4. Lacey, *Robert, Earl of Essex*, p. 49.

5. Sir Henry Wotton, *Reliquiae Wottonianae* (London, 1651), p. 28.

6. John Speed, *The History of Great Britaine* (London, 1611), p. 865. See also *A Brief Discourse of Warre*, in *The Works of Sir Roger Williams*, ed. John X. Evans (Oxford: Clarendon, 1972), p. 13.

7. *Roxburgh Ballads*, 1:572.

8. Peele, *Eclogue Gratulatorie* (1589), in *Works*, 1:226–227. Peele's poem attempts to counter rumors regarding the expedition's failure.

9. Sir Julian Stafford Corbett, *The Successors of Drake* (London: Longmans, Green, 1900), p. 19.

10. *Correspondence of Sir Henry Unton*, ed. Joseph Stevenson (London, 1847), pp. 72–73.

11. Roy Strong, in Appendix I (pp. 206–212) of *The Cult of Elizabeth*, prints the rosters of participants in the Accession Day tilts and Saint Elizabeth's Day tilts (November 19) from 1581 to 1602, and these provide the data for my calculations and comparisons of frequency of appearance. During the 1590s Essex and his cohorts were surpassed in the number of appearances in the tiltyard by only two other peers: the Earl of Cumberland, who was the Queen's champion, and Lord Compton, whose passion for conspicuous consumption has already been noted. For a discussion of the roles of Bedford, Southampton, Sussex, and Mountjoy in the Essex conspiracy, see Lacey, *Robert, Earl of Essex*, pp. 250–51, 271–272.

12. Wotton, *Reliquiae Wottonianae*, p. 48.

13. Peele, *Polyhymnia* (1590), in *Works*, 1:235–36.

14. G. C. Williamson, *George, Third Earl of Cumberland* (Cambridge: Cambridge University Press, 1920), p. 168.

15. Strong, *Cult of Elizabeth*, p. 140.

16. Devereux, *Lives and Letters*, 1:188.

17. Wotton, *Reliquiae Wottonianae*, pp. 48—49.

18. Cyril Falls, *Mountjoy: Elizabethan General* (London: Odhams Press, 1955), p. 24.

19. *CSP, Domestic*, Elizabeth, 2:33.

20. Camden, *Annales*, pp. 552—553.

21. Francis Bacon, *Works*, 8:362; hereafter cited in the text.

22. Rowland Whyte to Robert Sydney, *Letters and Memorials of State*, ed. Arthur Collins (London, 1746), 1:362.

23. Strong, *Cult of Elizabeth*, p. 141.

24. C. G. Cruickshank, *Elizabeth's Army* (1946; Oxford: Oxford University Press, 1966), pp. 266, 268—269.

25. Thomas Birch, *Memoirs of the Reign of Queen Elizabeth* (London, 1754) 2:81, 96—97.

26. G. B. Harrison, *The Life and Death of Robert Devereux, Earl of Essex* (New York: Holt, 1937), p. 162.

27. Jonathan Marwil emphasizes Bacon's failure to understand his patron's character or situation, and he suggests that the Earl may never even have seen the letter, in *The Trials of Counsel: Francis Bacon in 1621* (Detroit: Wayne State University Press, 1976), pp. 82—83. Bacon's advice is more self-serving than solicitous, and it may be part of an attempt to cover his own flanks.

28. *HMC, Salisbury* (London, 1899), 9 (vii): 520.

29. Cecil Papers, Hatfield, 176, fol. 10r. These formulaic phrases actually apply to the monarch, a point Essex may have missed when skimming the draft.

30. The Earl's "eulogy of England's nobility and her aristocratic society" (p. 141) was recorded by William Camden in his commonplace book, now in the Beinecke Library at Yale University. Camden attended the trial as Clarenceux King of Arms. William Huse Dunham prints and discusses portions of the Earl's speech in "William Camden's Commonplace Book," pp. 151—152.

31. Robert W. Kenny, *Elizabeth's Admiral: The Political Career of Charles Howard, Earl of Nottingham, 1536—1624* (Baltimore: Johns Hopkins University Press, 1970), pp. 208—210.

32. *HMC, Salisbury*, 9 (vii): 527. Following Birch (*Memoirs*, 2:365), Robert Kenny says this complaint refers to Nottingham's letters patent, which both say Essex wanted to have altered (*Elizabeth's Admiral*, pp. 208—210). However, as the letter to Cecil indicates, Essex also wanted his own changed, and he may have assumed Nottingham opposed this as well.

33. *HMC, Salisbury*, 9 (vii): 527.

34. I searched for a record of Essex's creation as Earl Marshal in the Calendar of Privy Seal Warrants and the Calendar of Letters Patent, with the assistance of Mr. Norman Evans of the Public Record Office, and found no trace of it.

35. Birch, *Memoirs*, 2:365.

36. The Duke of Norfolk's two *Treatises on the Earl Marshal of England* assign command of the Royal Army to the Earl Marshal and the Constable. See Starkey, "Stewart Serendipity," p. 39.

37. BL Cotton MS, Vespasian 114, fol. 100r.

38. College of Arms, Vincent MS 99, fols. 175r, 179v.

39. Birch, *Memoirs*, 2:365.

40. Folger Library MS V.b.7, fol. 64. For a discussion of Henry Howard's efforts to continue the reforms initiated by his brother, see Linda Levy Peck, *Northampton: Patronage and Policy at the Court of James I* (London: Allen & Unwin, 1982), pp. 117–118.

41. Ibid., fols. 11–12. By "civilians" Howard means the civil lawyers. The High Court of Chivalry under the Earl Marshal's jurisdiction was regarded as a court of civil law, beyond the jurisdiction of common law; see G. D. Squibb, *The High Court of Chivalry* (Oxford: Clarendon Press, 1959), pp. 12–13.

42. BL Cotton MS, Vespasian 114, fol. 103v. The "one learned frend" responsible for "marshalling" all this research may have been William Camden, the newly appointed Clarenceux King of Arms and founder of the Society of Antiquaries, who also wrote two papers on the earl marshalcy. Linda Levy Peck has suggested to me that the "learned frend" might have been Lord Henry Howard. She discusses Howard's antiquarian interests and connections to Essex in *Northampton*, pp. 11, 13–18.

43. BL Cotton MS, Vespasian 114 (ii), fol. 106v.

44. Ibid.

45. Thomas Hearne, *A Collection of Curious Discourses* (London, 1771), 2:82, 83.

46. Thomas F. Mayer, "Faction and Ideology: Thomas Starkey's *Dialogue*," *Historical Journal* 28 (1985): 1, 25.

47. Thomas Starkey, *A Dialogue Between Reginald Pole and Thomas Lupset*, ed. Kathleen M. Burton (London: Chatto & Windus, 1948), pp. 165, 166.

48. John Ponet, *A Short Treatise of Politic Power*, in Winthrop S. Hudson, *John Ponet (1516?–1566): Advocate of Limited Monarchy* (Chicago: University of Chicago Press, 1942), p. 106.

49. See John Guy, "The King's Council and Political Participa-

tion," in Alistair Fox and John Guy, *Reassessing the Henrician Age: Humanism, Politics and Reform, 1500–50* (Oxford: Basil Blackwell, 1986), pp. 121–147, and David Starkey, "Stewart Serendipity," p. 49. Dr. Starkey also discusses the aristocracy's control of the council in "The Lords of the Council: Aristocracy, Ideology, and the Formation of the Tudor Privy Council,"a paper presented at the annual convention of the American Historical Association, Chicago, December 1986. I am grateful to Dr. Starkey for sending me a copy.

50. James E. Farnell, "The Social and Intellectual Basis of London's Role in the English Civil Wars," *Journal of Modern History* 49 (1977): 647.

51. Kevin Sharpe, *Sir Robert Cotton, 1586–1631: History and Politics in Early Modern England* (Oxford: Oxford University Press, 1979), pp. 28–29.

52. Birch, *Memoirs*, 2:385, 390, and *CSP, Domestic*, V (1598–1601), ed. Mary Anne Everett Green (London, 1869), pp. 88–89.

53. Wotton, *Reliquiae Wottonianae*, p. 23. Wotton says that Essex was never interested in "the reputation of a Courtier, ... though he had such places of honor and attendance as be the most significant badge of a Courtier" (p. 42).

54. Camden, *Annales*, p. 494.

55. Lacey, *Robert, Earl of Essex*, pp. 224–225.

56. *HMC, Salisbury*, IX, ix (London: HMSO, 1902), p. 10.

57. Harrison, *Robert Devereux*, pp. 238–239.

58. *HMC, Penshurst*, ed. C. L. Kingsford (London: 1934), 2:435.

59. See Arthur M. Hind, *Engraving in England in the Sixteenth and Seventeenth Centuries: The Tudor Period* (Cambridge: Cambridge University Press, 1952), 1:245–46. The other Earls were Cumberland, Nottingham, and Mountjoy. The last portrait may have been done in 1604 after Mountjoy's elevation to Earl of Devonshire, but the others were done between 1598 and 1599, predating the Act of the Privy Council suppressing such portraits. See Hind, 1:239, 243–46, 249. F. J. Leavy has called my attention to the dangerously imperial connotations of the image of the man on horseback; see Roy Strong, *Van Dyck: Charles I on Horseback* (New York: Viking, 1972), pp. 49–57.

60. 30 August 1600, *Acts of the Privy Council*, ed. John Roche Dasent (London: HMSO, 1905), n.s., 30:619–620.

61. Strong, *Cult of Elizabeth*, pp. 141, 211.

62. *HMC, Salisbury* (London: HMSO, 1904), 10:385.

63. *HMC, Penshurst*, 2:486.

64. Strong, *Cult of Elizabeth*, p. 211, and Williamson, *George, Third Earl of Cumberland*, pp. 242–243.

65. Strong, *Cult of Elizabeth*, p. 136.

66. Lacy Baldwin Smith, *Treason in Tudor England* (Princeton: Princeton University Press, 1986), pp. 197–198 passim.

67. James, *Society, Politics, and Culture*, p. 423.

68. William Barlow, *A Sermon Preached at Paules Crosse, on the First Sunday of Lent, Martii i, 1600. With a short discourse of the late Earle of Essex, his confession and penitence, before and at the time of his death*, quoted in James, *Society, Politics, and Culture*, p. 450.

69. *Correspondence of King James VI of Scotland with Robert Cecil and Others in England During the Reign of Queen Elizabeth*, ed. John Bruce (London, 1861), pp. 65–66. Even without being named Constable, Essex could still claim the powers of that office because of their joint jurisdiction in the Court of Chivalry; see James, *Society, Politics, and Culture*, p. 450.

70. Robert Parsons, *A Conference About the Next Succession to the Crowne of Ingland* (Antwerp?, 1594), sig. A 2v–3r.

71. Lacey, *Robert, Earl of Essex*, p. 133.

72. Ibid., p. 134. See also Neale, "The Elizabethan Political Scene," in *Essays in Elizabethan History*, pp. 80–81.

CHAPTER 5

1. Samuel Daniel, *Civil Wars*, p. 312; hereafter cited in the text.

2. Gascoigne, *Works*, 2:473.

3. See Laurence Michel's introduction to Daniel, *Civil Wars*, p. 30. Blount fell out of favor with King James after he and Penelope Rich, Essex's sister, sought to legitimate their relationship by marrying.

4. Jameson, *Political Unconscious*, p. 83.

5. Samuel Daniel, "Epistle Dedicatory," in *The Collection of the History of England*, in *Works*, 4:77; hereafter cited in the text.

6. Ibid.

7. Samuel Daniel, *The Tragedy of Philotas*, ed. Laurence Michel (New Haven: Yale University Press, 1949), p. 99; hereafter cited in the text.

8. Samuel Daniel, *Delia 46*, in *Poems and a Defence of Ryme*, ed. Arthur Colby Sprague (1930; Chicago: University of Chicago Press, 1965), p. 33; hereafter cited in the text.

9. Sidney, *Apology for Poetry*, p. 111.

10. Cecil Seronsy points out the incompatibility of these per-

spectives in "The Doctrine of Cyclical Recurrences and Some Related Ideas in the Works of Samuel Daniel," *Studies in Philology* 54 (1957): 387—389. R. B. Gill argues less persuasively that Daniel's writing only seems fatalistic in "Moral History and Daniel's *The Civil Wars*," *Journal of English and Germanic Philology* 76 (1977): 341—342.

11. See also the speech by the Chorus in Daniel's *Cleopatra*: "Ah no, the course of things requireth / change and alteration euer" (*Works*, 3:75) as well as Daniel's "Apology" in *Philotas*:

> These ancient representments of times past
> Tell us that men haue, doe, and alwayes runne
> The selfe same line of action, and doe cast
> Their course alike, and nothing can be done,
> Whilst they, their ends, and nature are the same.
>
> (p. 97)

12. For a discussion of Daniel's respect for the Middle Ages, see May McKisack, "Samuel Daniel as Historian," *Review of English Studies* 23 (1947): 226—243, and Clark Hulse, "Samuel Daniel: The Poet as Literary Historian," *Studies in English Literature* 19 (1979): 55—69.

13. Arthur B. Ferguson, "The Historical Thought of Samuel Daniel: A Study in Renaissance Ambivalence," *Journal of the History of Ideas* 32 (1971): 195.

14. G. M. Logan, "Daniel's *Civil Wars* and Lucan's *Pharsalia*," *Studies in English Literature* 11 (1971): 57.

15. See Frederick M. Ahl, *Lucan: An Introduction* (Ithaca: Cornell University Press, 1976), pp. 37—48, for a discussion of Lucan's relationship with Nero.

16. Lucan, *The Civil War (Pharsalia)*, trans. J. A. Duff (1928; Cambridge, Mass.: Harvard University Press, 1977), p. 614.

17. Ibid., pp. 401, 51.

18. Michel, Introduction to Daniel, *Civil Wars*, p. 33.

19. Lucan, *Pharsalia*, p. 263.

20. John Milton, *Paradise Lost*, in *Complete Poems and Major Prose*, ed. Merritt Hughes (New York: Odyssey Press, 1957), p. 379.

21. Thomas Traherne, *Christian Ethicks* (1675), chap. 28, quoted in Margaret Greaves, *The Blazon of Honour: A Study in Renaissance Magnanimity* (London: Methuen, 1964), p. 114.

22. "Epistle to Prince Henrie," in John Pitcher, *Samuel Daniel: The Brotherton Manuscript* (Leeds: University of Leeds Press, 1981), p. 135. See also Pitcher's discussion of this epistle, pp. 21—26.

23. Henry is advised not to go beyond "Alcides pillars," or the pillars of Hercules, ordinarily identified with Gibraltar. Daniel regards these as limits not to be crossed, invoking the same image in the last sentence of his *Collection of the History of England*; see Pitcher's discussion of this image in *The Brotherton Manuscript*, pp. 31–35.

24. Michel, Introduction to Daniel, *Philotas*, pp. 45–66.

25. James, *Society, Politics, and Culture*, pp. 455ff.

26. Joan Rees, *Samuel Daniel* (Liverpool: Liverpool University Press, 1964), p. 104.

27. Quoted in Michel, Introduction to Daniel, *Philotas*, pp. 38–39.

28. Ben Jonson, "Epistle to John Selden," in *The Complete Poetry of Ben Jonson*, ed. William B. Hunter, Jr. (1963; New York: Norton, 1968), p. 145.

29. These are prefatory verses to the 1607 edition of his poems entitled *Certaine Small Workes*.

CHAPTER 6

1. Edmund Spenser, *A View of the Present State of Ireland*, ed. W. L. Renwick (1934; Oxford: Clarendon Press, 1970), p. 168.

2. Yates, *Astraea*, p. 97.

3. Norbrook, *Poetry and Politics*, p. 109.

4. Richard Helgerson, *Self-Crowned Laureates: Spenser, Jonson, Milton, and the Literary System* (Berkeley: University of California Press, 1983).

5. Sidney, *Apology for Poetry*, p. 124.

6. Alpers argues very persuasively that Spenser's "claim to relative autonomy, by means of something that looks like aesthetic 'space,' was Spenser's historical (and therefore, indeed, problematic) aim in *The Shepheardes Calender*" (Paul Alpers, "Pastoral and the Domain of Lyric in Spenser's *Shepheardes Calender*," *Representations* 12 [1985]: 94).

7. Burke, *Philosophy of Literary Form*, p. 298.

8. "Three Proper and Wittie Familiar Letters," in Spenser, *Poetical Works*, p. 628.

9. Virginia Stern, *Gabriel Harvey, His Life, Marginalia, and Library* (Oxford: Clarendon Press, 1979), p. 43.

10. *Have with You to Saffron-Walden*, in *The Works of Thomas Nashe*, ed. Ronald B. McKerrow (1903; Oxford: Basil Blackwell, 1958), 3:76–78.

11. Thomas Hugh Jameson, "The *Gratulationes Valdinenses* of Gabriel Harvey," Ph.D. diss., Yale University, 1938, p. 65.

12. "Three ... Letters," in Spenser, *Poetical Works,* p. 612.

13. John Florio, *Second Frutes* (1591; Gainsville, Fla.: Scholars' Facsimile and Reprints, 1953), sig. A 3v.

14. Ibid., sig. A 3r.

15. "Two Other Very Commendable Letters" and "Three ... Letters," in Spenser, *Poetical Works,* pp. 635, 612.

16. Norbrook, *Poetry and Politics,* p. 84.

17. Patrick Cullen, *Spenser, Marvell, and Renaissance Pastoral* (Cambridge, Mass.: Harvard University Press, 1970), p. 114; Thomas H. Cain, *Praise in "The Faerie Queene"* (Lincoln: University of Nebraska Press, 1978), p. 17; and Louis Montrose, "The Elizabethan Subject and the Spenserian Text," in *Literary Theory/Renaissance Texts,* ed. Patricia Parker and David Quint (Baltimore: Johns Hopkins University Press, 1986), pp. 321–322.

18. Montrose, "Elizabethan Subject," p. 323.

19. Yates, *Astraea,* p. 101.

20. See Michael Leslie, *Spenser's "Fierce Warres and Faithfull Loves": Martial and Chivalric Symbolism in "The Faerie Queene"* (Cambridge: D. S. Brewer, 1983), pp. 138–146, as well as Josephine W. Bennett, *The Evolution of "The Faerie Queene"* (Chicago: University of Chicago Press, 1942), pp. 39ff.

21. Rosemond Tuve, *Allegorical Imagery* (1966; Princeton: Princeton University Press, 1977), p. 355.

22. On the endlessness of romance in general and *The Faerie Queene* in particular, see Michael Murrin, *The Veil of Allegory: Some Notes Toward a Theory of Allegorical Rhetoric in the English Renaissance* (Chicago: University of Chicago Press, 1969), p. 101; Patricia Parker, *Inescapable Romance: Studies in the Poetics of a Mode* (Princeton: Princeton University Press, 1979), pp. 56ff; and Jonathan Goldberg, *Endless Worke: Spenser and the Structures of Discourse* (Baltimore: Johns Hopkins University Press, 1981).

23. Richard Helgerson, "Tasso on Spenser, or the Politics of Chivalric Romance." I am indebted to Richard Helgerson for sending me a copy of this unpublished paper.

24. Elizabeth J. Bellamy, "The Vocative and the Vocational: the Unreadability of Elizabeth in *The Faerie Queene,*" *ELH* 54 (1987): 1, 4, 6.

25. Maureen Quilligan, *The Language of Allegory: Defining the Genre* (Ithaca: Cornell University Press, 1979), p. 182. See also Quilligan, *Milton's Spenser* (Ithaca: Cornell University Press, 1983), p. 95.

26. Tuve, *Allegorical Imagery*, p. 52.

27. Anthea Hume, *Edmund Spenser: Protestant Poet* (Cambridge: Cambridge University Press, 1984), p. 155.

28. Norbrook, *Poetry and Politics*, p. 120.

29. John Dixon, *The First Commentary on "The Faerie Queene*," ed. Graham Hough (1964; Folcroft, Pa.: The Folcroft Press, 1969), pp. 7–11.

30. Norbrook, *Poetry and Politics*, p. 122.

31. Kenneth Gross, *Spenserian Poetics: Idolatry, Iconoclasm, and Magic* (Ithaca: Cornell University Press, 1985), p. 125.

32. Leslie, *Spenser's "Fierce Warres*," p. 177.

33. Ibid., pp. 168, 195.

34. Ibid., p. 183.

35. Greenblatt, *Renaissance Self-Fashioning*, p. 192. Greenblatt contrasts "Spenser's profoundly *undramatic* art" and allegory with Shakespeare's and Marlowe's more skeptical and critical works.

36. Angus Fletcher, *Allegory: The Theory of a Symbolic Mode* (1964; Ithaca: Cornell University Press, 1982), pp. 23, 189. Fletcher roots these conflicts in the problems of patronage, explaining that "patronage and the pursuit of patronage become matters that may entail the most violent conflicts of allegiance" (p. 272).

37. Gross, *Spenserian Poetics*, p. 56.

38. Ivan L. Schulze, "Reflections of Elizabethan Tournaments in *The Faerie Queene*, 4.4 and 5.3," *ELH* 5 (1938): 278–284.

39. Jonson, *Complete Poetry*, p. 7.

40. See Richard Neuse, "Book VI as Conclusion to *The Faerie Queene*," *ELH* 35 (1968): 329–353; Michael O'Connell, *Mirror and Veil: The Historical Dimension of Spenser's "Faerie Queene"* (Chapel Hill: University of North Carolina, 1977), pp. 183–184; David Miller, "Abandoning the Quest," *ELH* 46 (1979): 173–192; and Richard Helgerson, *Self-Crowned Laureates*, pp. 90–100.

41. William V. Nestrick, "The Virtuous and Gentle Discipline of Gentlemen and Poets," in *Spenser: A Collection of Critical Essays*, ed. Harry Berger, Jr. (Englewood Cliffs, N.J.: Prentice-Hall, 1968), p. 138.

42. Yates, *Astraea*, pp. 99–100, pp. 103–105.

43. Ibid., p. 101n.3, Yates prudently refrains from attempting "to formulate what the connection was or how it worked" (ibid.).

44. William Nelson, *The Poetry of Edmund Spenser* (1963; New York: Columbia University Press, 1965), p. 293. See also Thomas Cain's remarks on Spenser's "about-face" toward Elizabeth in the later books of *The Faerie Queene*, in *Praise in "The Faerie Queene*," p. 185.

45. Miller, "Abandoning the Quest," 188.

46. Thus, I agree with David Norbrook, who contends that Spenser's vision of the Graces is not a retreat from the public world to the private realm of imagination (*Poetry and Politics*, p. 146), rather than with Jonathan Goldberg, who sees the vision as essentially solipsistic (*Endless Worke*, p. 173), or with Kenneth Gross, who also calls it an image of "redemptive solipsism" (*Spenserian Poetics*, p. 218).

47. A. C. Hamilton, "Our New Poet: Spenser, 'Well of English undefyled,'" in *Theatre for Spenserians*, ed. Judith M. Kennedy and James A. Reither (Toronto: University of Toronto Press, 1973), p. 110, and Bellamy, "Vocative and the Vocational," pp. 23–24.

48. Carl J. Rasmussen accurately notes that Leicester is "not put in the best light" in this poem and remarks on the "mysterious tension between Spenser and Leicester" evident here and in *Virgil's Gnat*, in "'How Weak Be the Passions of Woefulness': Spenser's *Ruines of Time*," *Spenser Studies* 2 (1981): 167.

49. See Peter M. Sacks, *The English Elegy: Studies in the Genre from Spenser to Yeats* (Baltimore: Johns Hopkins University Press, 1985), pp. 53–54.

50. The question of authorship of Clorinda's "dolefull lay" has recently been reopened. Spenserians have generally assigned the poem to Spenser (see the *Variorum*, 7:500–505), a view I am still inclined to accept; but for an account of recent scholarship attributing the poem to Mary Sidney, see Josephine A. Roberts, "Mary Sidney," *English Literary Renaissance* 14 (1984): 435.

51. Paul Alpers, "Convening and Convention in Pastoral Poetry," *New Literary History* 14 (1982–83): 287.

52. Harry Berger, Jr., "Spenser's 'Prothalamion': An Interpretation," in *Essential Articles for the Study of Spenser*, ed. A. C. Hamilton (Camden, Conn.: Archon, 1972), p. 519.

53. Helgerson, *Self-Crowned Laureates*, p. 88.

EPILOGUE

1. Quoted in Alexander C. Judson, *The Life of Edmund Spenser* (Baltimore: Johns Hopkins University Press, 1945), p. 206.

2. Richard F. Hardin, *Michael Drayton and the Passing of Elizabethan England* (Lawrence: University of Kansas Press, 1973), p. 83.

3. Arthur Wilson, *Life of James I* (1653), quoted in Roy Strong, *Henry, Prince of Wales and England's Lost Renaissance* (London: Thames & Hudson, 1986), p. 153.

4. On Arundel's "predilection for chivalrous sports," see Strong, *Henry, Prince of Wales*, p. 48.

5. Edward Hyde, Earl of Clarendon, *History of the Rebellion*, ed. W. D. Macray (Oxford, 1888), 1:70. The portrait is in the Isabella Stewart Gardner Museum in Boston.

6. Sir Edward Waller, *Historical Discourses*, cited in Brian Manning, "The Aristocracy and the Downfall of Charles I," in *Politics, Religion, and the English Civil War*, ed. Brian Manning (London: Edward Arnold, 1973), p. 41.

7. Paul Christianson, "The Peers, the People, and Parliamentary Management in the First Six Months of the Long Parliament," *Journal of Modern History* 49 (1977): 575. See also his "The Causes of the English Revolution: A Reappraisal," *Journal of British Studies* 15 (1976): 40—75.

8. Vernon F. Snow, *Essex the Rebel, The Life of Robert Devereux, the Third Earl of Essex, 1591—1646* (Lincoln: University of Nebraska Press, 1970), p. 496.

9. Christianson, "The Peers, the People, and Parliamentary Management," p. 581.

10. See Laurence Michel's note on the parallels between this passage and Milton's *Areopagitica* in Daniel, *Civil Wars*, p. 356.

11. Milton, *Areopagitica*, in *Complete Prose Works*, 2:492.

12. Ibid., 2:555, 515.

13. John Milton, *Manso*, in *Complete Poems and Major Prose*, p. 130.

14. John Milton, *An Apology for Smectymnuus*, ed. Frederick L. Taft, in *Complete Prose Works*, 1:891.

15. Ibid.

Index

189

Compositor: Asco Trade Typesetting Ltd.
Printer: Braun-Brumfield, Inc.
Binder: Braun-Brumfield, Inc.
Text: 10/12 Palatino
Display: Palatino